THE
GOLDEN
RULES

THE
GOLDEN
RULES

*10 Steps to World-Class
Excellence in Your Life and Work*

BOB BOWMAN

COACH OF 18-TIME OLYMPIC
GOLD MEDALIST MICHAEL PHELPS

WITH CHARLES BUTLER

ST. MARTIN'S PRESS ≋ NEW YORK

www.stmartins.com

The Library of Congress Cataloging-in-Publication Data is available upon request.

ISBN 978-1-250-05950-5 (hardcover)
ISBN 978-1-4668-6457-3 (e-book)

Our books may be purchased in bulk for promotional, educational, or business use. Please contact your local bookseller or the Macmillan Corporate and Premium Sales Department at 1-800-221-7945, extension 5442, or by e-mail at MacmillanSpecialMarkets@macmillan.com.

First Edition: May 2016

10 9 8 7 6 5 4 3 2 1

*To Michael Phelps, whose willingness
to trust me and to challenge me is the
foundation of my journey.*

To all the swimming Butlers.

CONTENTS

FOREWORD

BY MICHAEL PHELPS

All I ever wanted to do was to compete at the Olympics. Bob Bowman made sure that dream came true—along with so many others.

Oh, for sure, I had something to do with getting to the Summer Games in Sydney, and then in Athens, and then in Beijing, and then in London. And if all goes according to plan, I'll be at the 2016 Olympics in Rio de Janeiro, too. For nearly twenty years, my days have begun with an early-morning swim practice—and another step toward fulfilling my competitive goals. And it's a rare day when Bob Bowman hasn't been there to meet me on the pool deck and to watch my every stroke and to call out my next practice set and, perhaps most important, to push me with that South Carolina accent of his—*"Michael, you can do better! Muuuuch better!"*—to get more out of my efforts than I ever thought possible.

With his coaching and, even more so, with his passion

for achieving excellence, Bob has shown me how far I can take my talents and my dreams.

Now, since the day of my first workout with Bob, his voice has mellowed and his hair has gotten grayer, which is a development I'll take some credit for. You see, Bob may be the greatest swim coach in the world, but that doesn't mean we've always seen eye to eye or that I've followed his Golden Rules to a tee. As in any relationship, we've had our high points and, well, our low points. Still, the record book tells a good part of our collective story: Over the course of four Games, we won 22 medals, including 18 gold medals; both are Olympic records. And now, going into the Rio Games, Bob and I have no reason to believe that we can't turn more dreams into reality.

While Bob's appearance and demeanor may have changed in subtle ways over the years, one thing hasn't: He remains committed to his step-by-step Method for achieving success and excellence in whatever area a person pursues. From nearly the moment Bob became my coach, he told me this would be our plan: He'd help me set my goals, he'd help me put a plan in place to get me toward meeting those goals, and then he'd help me stay focused on my target even when everything didn't go according to plan. As I came to learn, his Method always seems to work.

There may be many reasons why you've picked up this book. Maybe you have dreams like I once did of getting to the Olympics. Or maybe you want to become the best heart surgeon the world has ever known. Or maybe you need help in becoming a CEO or a concert pianist or simply the finest mom or dad possible. I can't assume to know your goal, but I do know this: You've come to the right place. Because if you are someone with a dream, and a desire to excel, then Bob Bowman's Method will work for you. Trust me.

Trust me. I can't believe I'm saying that when I can so easily remember how my relationship with Bob started. When I was ten years old and first saw him around my swimming pool in Baltimore, I said to myself, I'm never swimming for that man. He seemed almost possessed: constantly whistling and pacing up and down the pool deck and telling swimmers, "Step it up, *peeeeeo-ple!* We can do better, *peeeeeo-ple!*"

But within a year I was swimming in his group—and discovering that he was a coach like no other. He was always prepared, constantly planning not just for today but for tomorrow, and extremely devoted to achieving excellence in even the smallest of tasks. In the days and years that followed, I came to understand the wisdom of his ways.

As it turned out, something started to click between us within a few weeks of my joining his group. We were in a phase where if he said, *Jump!* I would say, *How high?* I didn't miss a beat. I did everything perfectly in practice. He told me what times he wanted me to go and I would just do them. Along the way I saw much progress toward my main goal. Like I said, I had always dreamt of making the Olympics and being a gold medalist and setting a world record. I just needed a map to get me there. One day, in the summer of 1997, Bob gave me that map. He had asked my parents and me to meet with him. At first I just figured I was in trouble for goofing off at a previous practice. Instead, he told us that I had a chance to set some special marks in the sport of swimming. He said things I wanted to hear. He said I could make not just one Olympic team but many Olympic teams. And when I eventually got to the Olympics, I would have the chance to win medals. He didn't guarantee anything, but he laid out the possibilities with a good deal of certainty.

For some reason, that day I decided to trust Bob with my career. I've never regretted the decision.

Four years later, I made my first Olympic team. I was fifteen years old. I didn't even have a driver's license. But as promised, Bob got me to do something pretty special. We went off to Sydney for the Games. I didn't medal that year, but Bob and I soaked up the atmosphere—and started looking ahead to the next Games. We returned to Baltimore and made a plan. Four years later I had my first gold medal, and another dream checked off.

Now, as it has turned out, along with my successes I've also had my setbacks, with some becoming very public ones. In times like these Bob, coach and friend, stayed with me and mentored me and, most of all, told me to push through a difficult today to set myself up for a better tomorrow. As he points out in *The Golden Rules*, excellence is the product of everyday effort. But not every day can be a gold medal–winning one. Hard times are part of the deal. Working through adversity is a component of "excellence training," and for teaching me that skill, I'm indebted to Bob.

The most lasting lessons often came when Bob and I were away from the pool. It's funny, but at big swim meets, even at the Olympics, Bob and I would never talk race strategy. We got that stuff out of the way back in Baltimore. No, in the downtimes at these events, we most often talked about life, and I learned things that I would store for future use, either when my race calendar was empty or when my swimming career finally came to an end.

If I have my way, that won't be anytime soon.

When I came out of retirement to train for the 2016 Olympics, it was because I still wanted to achieve things in the pool. But to do that, I needed to get back to training in the best way possible. That way is Bob's way. He is a master tactician. He can break a swim stroke down so that any swimmer, young or old, novice or Olympic-level, can understand the method behind the madness. But calling Bob a swimming tactician undervalues his true calling. He is a motivator and a teacher. He is someone who can take people with a passion and show them how far they can go with it. He's developed a formula for helping people go from one level to the next, and through his Method they learn more about who they actually are. In short, he makes people better.

I'm proof. Without Bob, my story is different—100 percent different. Without Bob, I have no shot at achieving the records I've achieved or winning the medals that I've won. I don't believe any other coach could have brought me to where I am today. Bob is one of a kind. He made me see the value of pursuing excellence and what it could bring. And what was that? No, not medals or records, but memories born of dreams.

THE
GOLDEN
RULES

I

A CHAMPION'S PURSUIT

Sometimes, when you stop for a moment to look ahead, the pause only keeps that list of things you need to get done from getting shorter, and it does little to shrink the number of people who are depending on you for something, and it certainly doesn't make all the bills that have piled up go away, because, well, the pause might also keep the checks from coming in. And when all this happens, when the twin monsters of Anxiety and Stress start pounding at your door, it's easy to put your hands up and say, "You got me, fellas. You win. I give up."

But on a gorgeous summer night back in 2013, with a setting sun skimming the white sand of the Delaware shoreline and an easy breeze whistling off the Atlantic Ocean, those monsters had no chance of catching me.

How could they? Just weeks earlier I had finished taking a few months off from work and competition and the daily grind. In a sense, I had taken off from life, and I was still feeling the rush. I had needed the break. For the better part of sixteen years, I had let the quadrennial Olympic cycle all but consume me—preparation for one Summer Games (Sydney) turning into preparation for the next (Athens), and that turning into the next (Beijing), and then the next (London). Oh, for sure, I loved the opportunities the Olympics brought me. The travel, the TV appearances, the passing out of Olympic pins in the different villages, the tossing back of the local brews—Foster's in Sydney, Tsingtao in Beijing, Newcastle in London. Great fun that came with enormous rewards.

But to achieve these magnificent moments I had to be willing to expend exceptional amounts of psychic energy. Understand, I'm not complaining. It's the deal with any job—banker, CEO, computer programmer, mother, father—where there are demands and deadlines and you're pursuing excellence while others may be content with "good enough." I knew that that kind of pressure was part of the formula for success: To achieve, and to achieve with distinction, sometimes you need to push harder than you had ever planned.

Now, though, with the next Olympics—Rio 2016—not that far away, I wasn't yet ready to let Anxiety and Stress get to me, even though I could feel them closing in as the to-do list got longer each day. Instead, I felt inspired by the challenges this cycle would bring me. New athletes to coach, new records to chase. Plus, after having gone through the quadrennial so many times, I knew what to expect and how to deal with just about anything the work brought.

And one more thing: I would be doing all this without the pressure of making the greatest Olympian of all time even greater.

So, as I looked out onto the Atlantic on this August evening, with a couple of teenage kids goofing off on their surfboards, and with some toddlers on the boardwalk smearing ice cream all over their parents' clothes, I realized one thing: That mounting pile of stuff on my desk and in my head had no power to break me.

And then my phone buzzed.

Hmm, I thought, looking down. I wonder what *he* wants.

"Let's have dinner soon. MP"

Simple, to the point, just like so many other messages he had texted me in the nearly two decades we had known each other, a period during which we had pushed each other to break records, win medals, and achieve greatness—and pushed our friendship to extreme heights and, at points, to severe peril.

But, as I had also come to know over that time, nothing is ever that simple when it involves MP—Michael Phelps.

A few days later, I met Michael at the Four Seasons Hotel in Baltimore's Inner Harbor. He had made a reservation for the two of us at Wit & Wisdom, one of the finest and priciest restaurants in the city.

"You're paying," I told him as we sat down.

I hadn't seen much of him of late; in fact, our paths had crossed only a few times since the conclusion of the London Olympics the previous summer. At those Games, Michael cemented his stardom for all time by winning the last of his record-setting twenty-two Olympic medals, then told the world he was retiring to go make Subway commercials, travel the world, and play a lot of golf. You know, the typical life of every twenty-seven-year-old. Me? I had a mortgage still to pay, a payroll to meet, and some more athletes who wanted to see if I could coach them to become the next superstar. I was forty-seven years old and in no position to retire. But I also knew that I needed some time away to refresh and assess where I was and where I wanted to go next. So, for nine months or so, I hung out at the racetrack watching the thoroughbreds, I relaxed at the beach, I read a lot of books, I watched too much Food Network, and, most of all, I paused and looked ahead.

During that post-London period, Michael and I called each other now and then and we'd see each other at the occasional Baltimore Ravens football game or at a charity event. But after being together through four Olympics—which meant thousands of hours of preparation at our "office" (our training pools in Baltimore) and crisscrossing the world to compete at swim competitions—we needed a break from each other.

By no means, though, was this a breakup.

We were business partners, and we had plans to open

swim schools around the world in the coming years. We were also in talks with a manufacturer to design and develop a new type of racing suit. Big jobs, for sure, but not so deadline-driven that they couldn't wait a bit. Plus, the way I saw things, those jobs had nothing on my previous one: making Michael the greatest Olympian of all time.

While Michael and I waited for the sommelier to arrive, we small-talked. He asked about my latest misadventures in the kitchen; those Food Channel shows had hooked me on trying to become an amateur chef. He told me about his latest trials with his putter. "Bob, I'm driving fine, chipping perfectly," he said. "I just can't read the greens. It's driving me crazy." I knew the feeling. Our last few years of Olympic training had tested our friendship, and my sanity. And the memories were still raw. We wanted to end Michael's Olympic run with a flourish, and we eventually did. Getting there, though, took a physical and mental effort on my part that I couldn't imagine ever repeating.

But tonight, I told myself, I wouldn't dredge up the past. I took a breath and, with my glass filled with a nice Merlot, sat back and relaxed . . . for maybe half a second.

Michael leaned forward and his eyes narrowed. He looked at me and said, "I'm thinking about coming back." I stared at him. He smiled a bit. "Yep," he went on, "I'm thinking about the Olympics one more time."

I wasn't sure if I should jump for joy or start crying.

"You want to come back?" I asked, a bit shocked and confused. He sort of grinned and nodded.

Maybe I shouldn't have been so surprised. A few months earlier, while he was on vacation with some buddies in Cabo San Lucas, Michael had called me late one night and started blathering on about making some sort of return. At the time, I didn't think much of the call; I simply took it as a late-at-night-Michael ramble and told him, "Absolutely not," and hung up.

But on this night, as he sat across the table from me, I could tell he was serious. And I wondered, Why? Why would he want to go through all the effort of another Olympic cycle? Michael had legendary status: eighteen Olympic golds among his twenty-two total. He'd broken dozens of world records and made millions of dollars along the way. The press had scrutinized nearly every angle of his short life; a comeback would put the media back on his trail. Plus, had he forgotten the run-up to the London Olympics and how miserable both he and I were?

"Do you remember those last four years?" I finally asked him.

"It won't be like that," he said.

"Yeah, sure," I said. "I've heard that before." Then I shook my head.

There was silence for a minute or so. I thought about what his decision would mean, for him and for me. Then I said, "If you're making a comeback for your sponsors, or if you're doing it because you don't have anything better to do with your life, or if you can't figure your life out, then you should not do it. Michael, I mean it: You should not do it."

He nodded. And waited. Then he said, "Bob, I can tell you, those aren't the reasons."

I came at him again. "Let me be clear, Michael. Unless you're doing it for the right reasons, and those reasons have to be that you're doing it only for yourself, then you should not do this."

Now, for the first time all night—in fact, for the first time that I could remember—Michael looked at me with the face of a wizened young man. And he said, "That's the only reason I want to do it. For me. I love to swim. I want to swim."

He paused for a second. "And I have more things I want to accomplish."

That's when I knew for certain that he meant what he was saying—and, better yet, that much of what I had sought to teach him over the years, beyond an explosive freestyle stroke or a killer flip turn, had taken root. Yes, in a matter of a few minutes, my life had suddenly become more complicated. I knew that along with Anxiety and Stress, Michael would be making a comeback, too. But that was okay, because it meant that I was once again in the business of working with someone who knew how to dream big and also knew what it took to make such a dream real.

Michael wasn't coming back to win medals; he was coming back to *achieve* something. And, as we had so many times before, we would do it together. One stroke, one kick, one race at a time, a partnership in pursuit of excellence.

GETTING GOLD OUT OF EVERY DAY

Like a lot of the great teams and enterprises in sports, in business, in science, in music, in life, Michael Phelps and I have worked together to envision markers we wanted to reach in our careers and in our lives and then pushed damn hard to attain them. While others have done the same thing in laboratories and backyard garages, in high-rise office towers and small shops along Main Street, USA, we just happened to do much of our work within the confines of a pair of 50-meter pools on the outskirts of downtown Baltimore.

And one more thing made us somewhat unique: We followed a process that I call, simply, the Method.

It's a ten-step plan that I first started testing when Michael wasn't yet a teenager, but I guess you could say it worked out pretty well. And I believe it can work just as well in the boardroom, in a retail shop, in the family kitchen as it did in our swimming venues. Anywhere achievement and excellence are sought, the Method can work. And it can work even if you don't have Olympic dreams or a Bob Bowman charting your day-to-day efforts.

Sure, you might be saying, the Method works because this guy Bowman coached the greatest natural-born swimmer ever. Well, Michael may be a freakishly talented athlete and he may be the most prominent swimmer I've ever worked with, but come visit me in Tempe, where I now head up the Arizona State University swimming program, or the Meadowbrook Aquatic & Fitness Center, my pool in Baltimore. You'll see plenty of photos spotlighting the other Olympic-medal winners who have worked through my process. And I'm confident that my system works out of the pool as well as it does in the pool. It's not intended simply to turn a good swimmer into a gold medal–winning one. It's meant to motivate a person to pull greatness— to get gold—out of every day. In the pages that follow, I'll lay out the Method and show you how it can work for you.

To be honest, the Method uses a simple formula. Together with an athlete or one of my employees, I break things down, then look to build them up. We set plans to follow by the day, the week, the month, and the year, along with desired outcomes. We butt heads. Lord knows we butt heads. (There are lots of stories about how Michael and I yelled and screamed at each other along the way to twenty-two medals—and you know, some are even true; I'll share a few of them shortly.) But most of all we focus on a target, and we never let that target out of our sight.

In Michael's case, for this process to take hold he had to realize that he could be more than a good swimmer; he could be world-class. And I had to realize that I needed to work even harder to take him from respectable to wondrous. No shortcuts permitted by either of us.

Here's one snapshot of how the Method works: It's the story of how I helped transform Michael's sloppy butterfly stroke into the greatest one ever. Now, don't get hung up on the tactical, "insider swimming" stuff. What this story reveals is how the use of a carefully orchestrated yet adaptable plan can bring success, whether you're a swimmer with the potential for Olympic greatness or someone just seeking greatness out of day-to-day life. It's the story of staying focused—something we all need to do to succeed.

It starts one day in the spring of 1997, when Michael was eleven and he was practicing with a group of kids about his age. That morning I immediately spotted a major flaw in his butterfly. It had to do with his breathing—specifically, the timing of when he took a breath. Sure, Michael may be an amazing physical specimen, but even he needed to get air into his body when racing 50 or 100 or 200 meters of butterfly, perhaps the most strenuous stroke in the sport. In Michael's case, he had a sort of a hiccup when taking a breath. He'd lift his head too far out of the water. I would tell him, "Don't pick your head up until your hands are under your waist. That will keep you from lifting your head too soon."

Think about that for a second. Seems doable, right? That is, until you jump into a pool and have a go at it.

And there was more instruction to come: "Michael, when you do go for a breath, just set your chin on top of the water and put it right back down."

In a way, these were small tweaks that the typical sports

fan would never notice. In reality, they were absolutely altering his stroke. The changes took weeks and months of practice to perfect. Through the Method Michael would get tired of hearing me repeat the commands. I would see him lift his head too far out of the water and scream, "No! Michael! Remember, Michael, just lift the chin!"

Like any eleven-year-old, he'd get frustrated. "Oh, yeah!" he'd blurt out, and then bang his fist on the surface of the water.

I'd prod; Michael would push back. I'd nudge; Michael would practice. The instruction came in a loop. Wash, rinse, repeat.

But it was through that cycle of instruction and repetition that success finally came.

And then greatness.

Within four years, by the time he was fifteen, Michael had set the world record for the 200-meter butterfly. Think about it. In the decades during which swimming records have been kept, decades that featured such stars as Johnny Weissmuller and Mark Spitz, no man had ever swum 200 meters of butterfly faster than this fifteen-year-old. How come? Because he took a plan and worked it.

I believe that's the power of the Method: everyday pursuit of excellence to achieve long-term greatness.

But Michael didn't just become a world-record holder on that day. Too many athletes and performers, and people in general, think the court or the stage or the podium in front of a sales team is where they really shine. The fact is, your most critical performances must take place away from the crowds and the lights and the expectant public. Michael produced that first world record—the first of thirty-nine he would set—because of all the mundane workouts he put himself through during the early-morning swim practices at an off-the-beaten-path pool in Baltimore. We practiced twice a day, at 7 A.M. before school and again for three hours after classes ended, in a pool where the only thing to focus on was the black lane line running its length. Swimming isn't like baseball or golf, where you're out in the sunlight and checking out the views across the field and getting a nice tan. No, with swimming you're wet, underwater, and using lots and lots of raw muscle power. And any improvement you make comes in milliseconds, not minutes. (Sound familiar? Anyone who has logged time in Cubicle Village, developing and then redoing PowerPoint presentations or monthly sales forecasts, can understand the swimmer's slog.)

Michael struggled through many of those practices; I know, because I was with him for nearly every one. I saw how his breathing would be right one day but then fall apart by the next. And I would remind him and pester him, and he would look at me in disgust. But he never stopped listening, trying, and hoping to perfect.

Finally, when he got the stroke, when his breathing was just about right, I assured him, "Michael, you now have it in the bank forever."

And I was right. Over the course of his first four Olympics, Michael competed in sixteen events in which he swam butterfly. He won a medal fourteen times.

But I will say this often in the pages that follow: We were not chasing medals; medals were just the tangible rewards. We were chasing excellence, and we achieved it often, and, in the process, gained even more: an appreciation for each other that would sustain itself long after his swimming career ended. Here's what I mean: Just before Michael's final race in London—at the time, we thought it would be his final Olympic race ever—I saw him in the practice pool, warming up, psyching up. He was aware of what was approaching, and so was I. I walked over to the side of the pool where he was now just hanging out. Through his goggles he must have seen me coming. I bent down, but before I could say a word Michael whispered through the din of the aquatic center, "Bob, I wanted to be like Michael Jordan in basketball and change the sport. Bob, I wanted people to know about swimming. We've done that, Bob. We've become the best ever, but we got here together. Bob, thanks. Thank you so much."

He caught me off guard, and I started to well up. "That's not fair," I said seconds later.

"I know," he said. "You can't see my tears, but yours are streaming down your face."

You see. That's an achievement that will last forever, one that doesn't need a medal to commemorate it.

ALWAYS SEEK EXCELLENCE—EVEN WHEN CHALLENGED

I'm frequently asked by companies to talk to their employees and to share the Phelps-Bowman secrets of success. Essentially, what I deliver is a condensed version of what's to come in the pages ahead. One thing I make clear in these talks is that the Method does not work overnight; it requires sustained effort. That said, it also challenges you every day, pushing you to improve on something, to set intermediate goals on the way to the big kahuna, and, most of all, to not settle. A few months back, one high-tech company—it's No. 1 in its category—invited me to talk to its best salespeople. They were the Michael Phelps of salesmanship. What could a swim coach tell them about selling? Well, this: "Whatever you do, avoid complacency. If you're already number one, set the bar higher, every day."

And that's where the parallel between Michael and you—the everyday man or woman—comes in. You might not stand six feet four inches with a wingspan that can gobble up water by the bucketful. You may not even have Olympic dreams. You might just want a promotion at the office, with a raise that will get you closer to owning that summer cottage in the woods. Or you're after an A in organic chemistry, which will look awfully good on your application to Harvard Medical School.

You have ambitions you want to realize, just like Michael.

The Method will do for you what it did for Michael. Compel you to raise the bar every day, a little or a lot. To shoot for excellence whenever possible.

I know. Achieving excellence every day sounds impossible. In fact, it's incredibly hard, mostly because of all the other stuff that gets in the way. Michael would be the first to agree with you, and here's proof: After the acclaim he received at the 2008 Beijing Games—remember, he won eight gold medals, the most ever by one person at an Olympics—he suffered a letdown; he needed to find something that would excite him, to recharge interest in a sport he'd been a part of since the age of five. As a result (and as I mentioned earlier), our relationship became contentious while he searched for this "something." For weeks and months, I didn't know when he would be ready to focus on the next big thing—and that's because *he* didn't know what that thing was. He avoided the pool, and when he did come by I couldn't help but nudge him about the upcoming London Games and the need to focus on it.

He took my prods like a bull reacting to a red cape.

"Nothing's good enough for you!" he barked at me more than once. "I had to win eight gold medals to get a 'Good job' out of you. Lay off, would you?"

To a certain extent, he was right. I would never accept anything less than his very best, and when he gave it I would reset to the notch above. That's the Method at work.

But I also knew that there comes a point in everyone's life when he must set his own course and plan his own process. The best coaches, the best bosses, the best parents, the best leaders are the ones who show their people not just how to get better but how to motivate themselves to get better.

Part of the Method—a very important part—is teaching people to deal with the inevitable challenges that come along during their daily lives. When I work with my swimmers, many of whom are teenagers or young adults, I give them daily obstacles to contend with. I challenge the men, for instance, to swim a hundred yards of freestyle in under fifty seconds when they're already exhausted from fifteen minutes of brutal sprints. Part of the exercise is to make them more physically ready for competition. But the training also prepares their psyches to handle the monsters—Anxiety and Stress—when they're either on the starting blocks of a major race or, more important, when they face an unforeseen hurdle in their personal lives.

Again, my relationship with Michael has provided me with a front-row seat for viewing the challenges he has had to confront outside the pool. As websites and the tabloids are more than happy to report, Michael's "real world" record hasn't always been golden. One too many times he's victimized himself with terrible judgment, leading to regrettable incidents that threatened to victimize others. I'm not about to condone some of his actions; the potential for harm they could have caused is without question. But I also know that his mistakes are reminders that there's perfection in gold, not in gold-medal winners. He has accepted the consequences of his lapsed judgment and is now using his experience to modify his daily life. In the coming pages, I'll show you how. The examples are as telling as any victory from his days at the Olympics.

GET PUMPED UP ABOUT YOUR PURSUIT

At that dinner when Michael told me about his comeback, he kept saying that he wanted this next Olympic cycle to be fun. Yes, he had goals to achieve, he told me, and he promised to work his tail off. But he also said that he wanted to enjoy the process as much as possible. I looked at him and smiled. "There's nothing wrong with that," I said.

Achieving excellence should not be drudgery. It should excite you; darn, you're going after something you want—savor every moment. As you'll see, the Method wants the process to be as satisfying as the reward is lasting. After nearly three decades of coaching athletes and other people, I've assembled strategies that, I believe, can lead anyone to personal fulfillment on the road to achieving his dream vision. Yes, effort is required, along with careful planning, the right attitude, teamwork, and a mentality that combats those monsters, Anxiety and Stress, when they close in. But they shouldn't diminish the joy of the chase.

The Method has worked for dozens of world-class swimmers—and I'm confident that it will work for non-swimmers as well, including you. It's part of my personal mission: to help people realize that the best moments in our lives are built around achieving everyday, and long-lasting, excellence.

So are you ready to pursue something special? Excellent. Let's go.

2

RULE 1: A CHAMPION SETS A "DREAM BIG" VISION

O n a warm, muggy, late-summer afternoon in Balti-more, a little before 2 P.M., a dozen present and future stars of swimming gathered in the cramped meeting space that overlooks the two 50-meter pools at the Meadowbrook Aquatic & Fitness Center. Before I relocated to Tempe in August of 2015, this space had been my home away from home, and on most days four staffers and I would shoehorn our way into the area, always careful not to nudge a Starbucks coffee onto an innocent laptop as we passed through the thin passageway between desks. At this moment, though, a group of gangly swimmers had taken up short-term residence. A tortoise has more elbow room in his shell than these athletes did that afternoon.

A pretty picture? Perhaps not. But the setting served my purpose.

Right then, the Method for planning and achieving some incredible dreams was about to begin. And, as I've come to learn, any dream worth going after often requires a bit of discomfort.

It was Tuesday, September 3, 2013, the day after Labor Day, and while most folks in the area were getting back into the routine of going to school and to work, these young men and women were preparing for something that was anything but routine. In a few minutes they would head downstairs, hop into our outdoor pool, swim 5,000 meters, and then do an hour's worth of gut-ripping dryland exercises. When that was over, they would head home for the night, relax, have dinner, and prepare for tomorrow and *10,000* meters of work.

In the scheme of things, today's workout wouldn't be anything especially over-the-top for these people; they had been swimming that kind of daily distance for years. But there was something different about today. It marked their first day on the road to fulfilling their long-held dreams of competing, excelling, and (if all went according to plan) achieving success at the Summer Olympics in Rio de Janeiro come August 2016.

Between this afternoon and the first Olympic heat, I had 1,068 days to prepare them—and each workout mattered.

Think back to the Olympic basketball Dream Team of 1992, with Michael Jordan, Magic Johnson, and Larry Bird. Or to the original cast of *Saturday Night Live,* with John Belushi, Dan Aykroyd, and Gilda Radner. Or to the tech geniuses of the recent past who have transformed our lives—Bill Gates, Steve Jobs, Jeff Bezos, Larry Page, and

Sergey Brin. Well, when it came to swimming, the team I was coaching, the North Baltimore Aquatic Club, had assembled a similar collection of all-stars, and at this moment they were all shoved into a tiny meeting space waiting to get to work.

There was Yannick Agnel, one of the greatest freestylers on the planet. The Frenchman had won two gold medals in the 2012 Olympics. He was perhaps the only swimmer in the world whom Michael might lose sleep over. For years he had trained with his national team in the picturesque French Riviera, but he had now moved to Baltimore to swim at "majestic" Meadowbrook, hard by a crusty hockey rink, an old train stop, and a run-down cotton mill. Another Olympic gold medalist, Conor Dwyer, had traded the palm trees, beaches, and year-round sun of Florida to train with me. There was the open-water Olympic gold medalist Oussama Mellouli. Originally from Tunisia, Ous had been working out at the University of Southern California for years. Now he was telling people he wanted to see what Bowman could do for him during his last Olympic go-round. Lotte Friis, one of Denmark's greatest champions ever, had relocated to the States, bringing her Danish warmth along with an Olympic bronze medal and multiple World Championships medals. Two recent college graduates and budding American stars—Virginia alum Matt McLean (a gold medalist at the 2012 Olympics in one of our relays) and North Carolina graduate Tom Luchsinger, who had just won a national title in butterfly—had moved to Baltimore to swim for me. Even a few high schoolers were on hand. They included Cierra Runge and Gillian Ryan, who would soon be making names for themselves on the collegiate and national stages.

And then there was perhaps the most inspirational of the lot: Jessica Long. Jessica, born in Russia and adopted by an American couple from suburban Baltimore, is a double below-the-knee amputee, which means that when she is in the pool ninety percent of her swimming strength comes from her arms and shoulders; she gets little from below the waist. Try swimming a few yards without using your legs; now think of Jessica and the thousands of yards she swims a day without them. Still, she is one of the most decorated Paralympic swimmers in history; she has seventeen medals, including twelve gold. At her pace, she could surpass Michael's haul one day. But, at that moment, sitting among these other stars who were now her teammates, and having moved to Baltimore from Colorado Springs to swim, she held out hope that I could get her somewhere that only dreams in the middle of the night had previously taken her.

Yes, a United Nations of swimming talent had been assembled. A Who's Who of pool hoppers. And that was with a couple of stars missing, including Allison Schmitt. Schmitty, as everyone called her, had been swimming for me since she was sixteen. I knew then what potential she possessed—but few others did, including Schmitty herself. At the Beijing Games, in 2008, she won a bronze medal.

Four years later, in London, and at the age of twenty-two, she won five medals, including three golds, and smiled her way into America's TV rooms. Now she was at the University of Georgia finishing her studies. She would rejoin my crew in a few months, as soon as she graduated. Chase Kalisz was also at Georgia, where he was starting his freshman year. He had been swimming at Meadowbrook since before he could spell *belly flop*. He may have been nine years younger than Michael, but as soon as he started showing up for workouts as a preteen he would try to race his idol over 25 meters—and sometimes even beat him. In a few months, he would set his first American record.

While Schmitty and Chase were not in Baltimore on this day, they had received an email from me days earlier, an email that told them it was time to start thinking ahead. Far ahead.

Oh, one other star was on hand this afternoon. His presence was a surprise to some. A big surprise. It was Michael. *But wasn't he retired?* A few of the other swimmers probably wondered. *Hadn't he told everyone after London that he was going to travel and play golf and sleep in?* They weren't yet aware of the dinner conversation Michael and I had had a couple of weeks earlier—or that Michael had come to realize that striking a little white ball wasn't enough to satisfy a twenty-eight-year-old who still wanted to squeeze more from his primary talent.

So, instead of hitting the links, MP was here to join his new teammates and to be part of the greatest swim team ever assembled outside of Olympic competition. A dozen men and women, each with personal pursuits. Each with a vision to do something very special.

And with me egging, jousting, leading them to where they wanted to go.

RULE 1.1: STAKE YOUR VISION ON WHERE YOU WANT TO GO.

Right from the start, understand this: There's nothing I love more than helping people fulfill their dreams.

A person could be in sales, in school, or in line to win an Olympic gold medal—it doesn't matter. As long as that person has a vision of what she wants to accomplish, I'll gladly offer my expertise on how she can reach her destination. And then I'll be with her, either in person or in spirit, once she begins that final leg toward a finish line. What if she needs a last-second push? Well, I'll give it to her, because I know what it takes to succeed and to achieve excellence, every day and throughout a career.

The Method begins with one essential ingredient: a vision. You need a vision of where you want to go, what you want to do, who you want to be someday down the road. Simply put: In your mind you must program your internal viewfinder toward a performance, toward an achievement, toward a scene that you see taking place in the future. Something you want to be a part of. That's your vision.

In part, that was the reason for this post–Labor Day meeting: I wanted these swimmers to crystallize the vision of their futures.

Without that vision, there is no starting point, no way to plan an attack. And no way to know whether or not you've achieved what you want to achieve.

Let me show you the power of vision.

RULE 1.2: USE FACTS (AND YOUR GUT) TO PLOT YOUR FUTURE.

It was a summer day in 1997. Michael was all of eleven years old but had already set several national age-group records. By then I had been a swim coach for more than a decade, though I had been around pools twice as long. And that experience led me to know that Michael, even as a seventh grader, was already doing something remarkable. I knew that he had places to go and even more greatness to achieve.

I had this vision, and it was based on facts, experience, and, yes, my gut.

Some salespeople sit by a humming Bloomberg terminal all day and then pore over *The Economist* come the weekend. They become so steeped in business trends that they can all but predict where the equilibrium point on the old supply-and-demand curve will fall without having to plug in any forecast numbers. They are students of their profession. It's the same thing with the best CEOs, like some of my heroes: Lee Iacocca, Steve Jobs, and someone many people may not know of, or, at least, not yet: Kevin Plank of Under Armour, the sports apparel company. These leaders saw the future because of what they did in the present: conversing regularly with their VPs; networking with fellow CEOs; getting out of their offices and viewing the changing business landscape. By collecting information and insights, they could anticipate challenges. The reward? Preemptive action that beat the competition. Iacocca saw the coming needs of soccer moms for vehicles that would tote traveling teams from town to town, so he brought out the Dodge Caravan. Jobs saw the rise in mobile technology, so he gave us the iPhone.

Kevin Plank, meanwhile, envisioned the surge in recreational sports among baby boomers—and brought to market triathlon and running gear to equip these aging but in-need-of-a-challenge athletes. I've visited Under Armour's headquarters several times; it's just a few miles from Meadowbrook. Each time I walk in I'm more impressed by the energy every employee exhibits and the collective vision they express. Under Armour's market share doesn't compare with those of Nike or Adidas—at least, not yet. But with Kevin's laserlike focus he's given his people a target—up!—to direct them.

Okay, I'm not comparing myself with Iacocca or Jobs or even Plank. I'm a swim coach, and in 1997 I was working with a bunch of preteens, many of whom came to practice simply because their dads and moms wanted them out of the house for a few hours. But while I may have been a glorified babysitter during some hours of the day, at other times I studied every swimming publication that came into the office. I tracked the names of kids in California and Ohio and Texas to see who was moving up in the ranks. I reviewed the practices that my mentors had used and the workouts that had shaped good swimmers into great ones. I went to conferences and soaked up the advice of fellow coaches. I submerged myself in swimming.

I was also a student of psychology and of what both motivates and inhibits people. I had studied psychology at Florida State University in the mid-1980s, receiving some of the finest insights into behavioral methodology a budding coach could ever want. I continued my research in the field after graduation, as I made my way up the coaching ranks and by moving all over the United States. In a ten-year span, I made more stops than a Greyhound bus crisscrossing the country. *Tallahassee. Cincinnati. Las Vegas. Birmingham, Alabama. Napa, California. Baltimore.* I called each city home at one point. But with each stop I learned something more about swimming techniques and even more about what makes people work, succeed, fail, adjust, and overcome. Every day was a Psychology 101 class.

All this research and experience fed something that was of even greater value to me: a vision I held for my own future. Ever since I had started in coaching, I sought to one day develop record-breaking swimmers. Not Olympic gold-medal swimmers but record-breaking swimmers. (I'll explain the difference in the next chapter.)

To achieve that dream, I needed to be ready when a potential record-breaker came within my circle. Eleven-year-old Michael Phelps—hyper, precocious, a cutup—fit just that profile.

My job: Get this kid, and those closest to him, to see the vision, too.

RULE 1.3: SUSPEND BELIEF TO SEE YOUR VISION.

With that in mind, on this August morning I invited Michael's parents, Debbie and Fred, to come to my office and to bring Michael with them. By this point I had been coaching Michael for just about four months. A good part of that time was spent corralling this wild pony. Out of the water the kid could drive you nuts with his Ricochet Rabbit antics. (At the age of nine, Michael was diagnosed with attention-deficit/hyperactivity disorder, or ADHD.) But when he was in the water focus replaced freneticism—an amazing trait, especially in someone so young. During practice he routinely beat kids older than him. And at meets he displayed signs of what would become a hallmark of his Olympic run: the capacity to concentrate under pressure. He'd stare the length of the pool, his mind set on one mission: going fast.

I had taught him a few lessons about pre-race focus, but, to be perfectly honest, he knew exactly what to do. He was a natural in so many ways.

Most of all, he had shown record-breaking talent, and this meeting would serve notice to Fred and Debbie—and

Michael, too—that they had to begin planning for what all this meant.

As the years pass, and as Michael's celebrity intensifies, the legend of this meeting has grown, especially with each retelling—I should say, with each Debbie retelling. During the past few Olympics, the world has gotten to know Debbie Phelps as Everyday Mom, the lovable, huggable, exuberant, quotable matriarch of Team Phelps who sat in her grandstand seat fidgeting and screaming while her son did extraordinary things in the water. The thing is, Debbie has trouble bottling that exuberance sometimes. When she goes out and gives talks to groups, she'll tell people that in this meeting I was like Carnac the Magnificent, the great seer, soothsayer, and sage made famous by Johnny Carson. She'll say that I laid out Michael's entire future at this meeting: that he would one day win twenty-two medals, set thirty-nine world records, appear on *Saturday Night Live*, inspire kids around the world to take up swimming, and, oh yes, get engaged to a Miss California USA.

Well, if I were that prophetic I would have been living in Vegas, not Baltimore.

But even with Debbie's recall being a touch off base, she's right about this: I did have a vision for her son, and I did see great things coming.

At this meeting, I told Debbie and Fred that we were dealing with a special talent; the times Michael was posting did not lie. I had crunched the numbers; I had compared times. I had researched what former eleven-year-olds had done, and what caused them to tail off later. That work made me more and more convinced that Michael's trajectory could be historic. I told them they needed to start planning ahead. In a sense they, like me, had to envision the future and prepare for it.

"Michael has real potential," I said. "I can see him doing things that no other swimmers can do."

Debbie and Fred weren't novices in competitive swimming. Their daughter Whitney had just missed making the 1996 Olympic team. But this was different. I was telling them that their middle-school son was an embryonic phenomenon. A sure thing not just to make an Olympic team but also to be competitive at future Games. Very competitive.

Debbie said, "Oh, no, he's too young."

I insisted. "Debbie, how are we going to stop it? It's not in our control," I told her. "Listen, I'm just telling you what's going to happen. In 2000, he'll be a factor at the Olympic Trials. I don't know if he'll make the team, but he's definitely going to make some noise." She looked at Fred; Fred looked at her. I was just beginning. "And by 2004," I went on, "he'll definitely be someone who will win medals in the Olympics. And it's only going to build from there."

No, I did not predict that he would win eight gold medals in 2008 and eclipse Mark Spitz's decades-old record for most golds by an athlete at a single Olympics. But I did see—and I told them this—that he could accomplish things never before seen in the sport.

As we would later discover, he surpassed even those expectations.

Before the meeting ended, Debbie looked at me for a good long time. Then she said, "You're crazy, Bowman."

Perhaps, but being a bit out there—suspending belief— is necessary when setting a vision for yourself or for those you work with. You want to establish a "reach," and then figure out a way to reach it.

RULE 1.4: DON'T JUST THINK ABOUT YOUR VISION. THINK ABOUT IT CREATIVELY.

It's easy to tell a young athlete that he needs a vision. Heck, it's easy to tell anyone—a co-worker, a best friend, a brother or sister—to have a vision. The reality is, establishing your vision requires work. You want to achieve something, right? In order to do that, you have to expend effort, and that starts with the vision phase.

In fact, to ignite the vision process I tell people that they need to *think creatively*. Notice, I'm not just saying think; I'm saying think creatively. Artists, musicians, writers, software developers are creative types. Ask them, and they will tell you that when they create, they work.

Here's how to start: Just find a spot where you're comfortable. It could be that old, beat-up but broken-in Barcalounger down in your basement. Or it could be a spot on your front stoop, the one with the best view of the setting sun. Or it could be atop that butte you climb early on a Saturday morning. Heck, it could be in the coffee shop where you sneak off for a long, workday lunch.

Wherever it is, go there. Thinking creatively requires a destination. A place where you can let your mind get to work.

I do this all the time. I have a beach house on the Delaware shore, and after a week of dealing with a bunch of ornery swimmers (or their parents) and employees who don't keep the pool deck as scrubbed as I would like or sportswriters who are looking for some gossip on Michael, I'll head out to the beach. I immediately grab my bike and go for a ride. The workweek instantly dissolves. When I get back home, I pour a glass of wine, head to my deck . . . and just start to think. For a moment, or more, I'm looking forward, not backward. I'm not thinking of all the emails that have already piled up in my in-box or of all the meetings that will be waiting for me come Monday.

I'm just asking myself, *Where am I now? Where could I go?*

Try it. Among my Method's ten steps to everyday excellence, this may be the easiest one. It costs no more than a few seconds, yet it's a major investment in your future.

In this step you're envisioning more than one thing. You're putting together a menu of a lot of things you want to do or become or achieve. Yes, you're fantasizing, but you're fantasizing with a purpose. Part of your thinking should include this subtext: "I may be dreaming, but this *could* happen."

Perhaps you're saying to yourself, "I want to have an apartment in Paris. And I want to be financially secure. And, while I'm at it, I even want to learn how to ski." Now, by the time the moment has passed you may realize that some of these visions are impossible to act on right now or in the next couple of months or even years. Maybe you still have a couple of kids going through middle school. Or maybe you have an aging parent whose health, you fear, is starting to slip. But there may be one vision among those that you could put on your immediate to-do list. For instance, who says you couldn't learn how to ski? Pick that one. It's a start toward something new.

Think this is all hogwash? Then you've never heard of Philip Levine. For years, starting at age fourteen, he worked at different auto plants around Detroit. He came home with fingernails crusty with grease and muscles that ached. He had plenty of reasons to just grab dinner, get ready for the next day in the shop, and fall into bed. Instead, he found time to envision the future that he wanted.

Levine wanted to be a poet. Don't you love that? A grease monkey with some Robert Frost in him. And he saw a purpose for his poetry: Through his verses he would tell the world about America's workers and what they did to get through their daily lives. He once told Terry Gross, the NPR host, "I actually thought that writing poetry would be a means of changing the world."

With that vision, Levine took the steps necessary to make his dream a reality. First off, he quit working in car plants. Then he started writing poems full-time. Rejection came, but so did acceptance. Eventually, he became a Pulitzer Prize winner and then served as poet laureate. Obviously, he accomplished quite a bit with his work, and Terry Gross later asked him if he had succeeded in changing the world. He admitted that he couldn't be sure, but he was certain of one thing: He had achieved his vision of becoming a poet. "[I]t was what I had to do," Levine said, "and whether it changes people or whether it doesn't, it's what I have to do."

RULE 1.5: PUT YOUR VISION DOWN IN WRITING.

The great thing about the vision step is that the number of permutations it produces is bounded only by your imagination. For example, take the different "vision quests" I've had during my life. As a kid, I was trained in classical piano and grew up dreaming that someday I would conduct a big-city orchestra, like one of my childhood heroes, Leonard Bernstein. So far, that vision hasn't turned into a reality—too many hours on a swim deck, I guess. But whenever I attend a concert I still look into the future and wonder.

More recently, with the next Olympics approaching, my visions typically have to do with swimming and my athletes. And with these visions I'm more likely to form a concrete plan of action. I'll sit on the deck of my beach house and envision one of my guys going 3 minutes, 42 seconds for the 400-meter freestyle. That's world-leading pace; it's also a steep improvement over where he currently stands. "If he can do that," I say to myself, "he's going to Rio and he'll be a serious contender once he gets there." On some nights, though, I dream about things that have nothing to do with eight-lane pools or stopwatches. For instance, I think of the thoroughbred horse I'm going to own one day that will bring me to the biggest racetrack in the world, Churchill Downs, and a spot in the Kentucky Derby. Or I'm picturing the golden, flaky crumb-apple pie I plan to bake for the huge Thanksgiving dinner I'm hosting in the fall.

You see, visions can come in all forms and contexts and, well, flavors and smells. One vision has to do with a bad-ass horse, another with an exquisite dessert, and another with an Olympic-level swimmer. What unites them is that they're mine. And the great thing about thinking creatively is that it's fun and revealing. You're seeing yourself in a different place, a place you want to be. A place you *can* be.

But you have to do more than just see your future. Remember, this step is an action-oriented one. I recommend that you codify your vision. For instance, after you've gotten fixated on a vision write a few words about it on a scrap of paper and tuck the paper in your wallet or in your desk. I tell all my swimmers to write down their vision—or, at least, to find some tangible way of reminding themselves of it. Tom Luchsinger, who's shooting to make the U.S.

team for the Rio Games in the butterfly, has a rendering of the five Olympic rings hanging from a doorway in his home. Each morning, before heading off to a workout, he gets a look at the rings—an instant reminder of why he's swimming 12,000 meters a day.

Another route: Tell someone (but not everyone) about your vision. I'm a big fan of this technique, because once you do, then you have someone in your corner. Someone who might help you get to where you want to go.

Here's a perfect example. Earlier, I mentioned Jessica Long, the Paralympic star. Before Jessica came to train with me, I knew of her, but I had never met her. That changed on a winter day in 2013. We had both been invited to Boston College to speak on a panel about leadership. After the session, I needed to rush to the airport to catch a flight. Just as I was about to get into the car that would get me there, Jessica called out to me, "Can I share a ride with you?"

"Sure," I told her, "jump in."

We made small talk as the car rushed through the Boston streets, but I could tell by her fidgeting that Jessica had something on her mind. Finally, just minutes from the airport, she cut to the chase. "Mr. Bowman," she started, "I have this dream of swimming in the U.S. Olympic Trials—not the Paralympic Trials, but the trials for everyone else." She blurted all that out in the same breath. It floored me. This was not the pronouncement I had expected to hear at that moment. She kept going. "No para-swimmer has ever made the Trials. I want to be the first. Can you coach me and get me there?"

I knew the times she would need to make the Trials; in some events, she would need to slice off as many as five seconds from her previous bests to even get close. And, eyeing the prosthetics attached to her knees, I knew the physical challenges she faced. Making the Trials? Her chances were slim.

That said, in the hour or so that I had spent with her, on the panel and now in the car, I had come to know a young woman who had already withstood and achieved so much. Birth defects. Orphanages. Life in a new country. Now here she was, pitching her idea, proclaiming her vision, with a smile so bright it made a cold Boston afternoon seem a lot warmer. Am I going to tell her "No go"?

"Jessica, give me a call when you get home," I said. "Let's talk more. This sounds intriguing."

A few months later, Jessica had relocated to her hometown of Baltimore and was swimming at Meadowbrook with some of the best able-bodied athletes in the world—and keeping up with them, for the most part. When she wasn't swimming, she was sharing something with them: her vision for her future.

Be like Jessica and envision something you would really like to achieve. Maybe you want to run your first marathon or go back to school to get a master's degree. Let a friend or a mentor know about this dream—someone you trust and someone who will encourage you to stay on track as you work toward your vision.

Or, if you're a corporate manager or the coach of a team, tell someone you work with about Jessica. What an inspiration you'll be sharing. Consider, for instance, that employee you supervise who is suddenly at the midpoint of her career. For years, she has done nothing but excellent work, but it is all the same work. Tell her you want to grab lunch. Find a day when there is no pressing need to rush back to the office. Over lunch, ask her, *What professional dream do you have for the next year or two? What do you want to accomplish? How do you see your role changing?* Maybe she'll say she's happy doing exactly what she's doing. Maybe, though, she'll share a vision that will not only challenge her and allow her to grow as a person but, if realized, could mean growth opportunities for your business as well.

Dream. And get the people around you to dream. And to see the future as Jessica Long does—with lots of possibilities.

RULE 1.6: YOUR VISION WILL PROVIDE THE PICTURE FRAME FOR FUTURE SUCCESS.

The question I'm often asked by the people I meet—whether they're swimmers I'm recruiting to Arizona State or new swimmers at my program in Baltimore or business executives I run into at the seminars I give—is *How do I know when I have a vision that is truly achievable?*

It's a good question but not an easy one to answer.

Predicting outcomes is tough business. In recent years I've become a big horse-racing fan, and I've come to know the tendencies of many thoroughbreds and what track conditions can mean to a particular horse and what tricks the best railbirds use to get an edge at the betting window. All that said, most days I still come home from the track with a lighter wallet than when the day started.

Results are impossible to know in advance. What is easier to nail down, though, is the "thing" you want to go after. Then, once you have that thing in mind, you can plan the road map toward achieving it.

History suggests that the predictions I made in that epic meeting with Michael and his parents fell well short of Michael's actual achievements. Still, we needed a framework to shape our long-term plan. A vision gives a purpose to daily pursuits. A reason to push yourself out of bed each morning and do something. Without this purpose, it's easy to drift through the days and weeks and months of life.

After that meeting broke up, Team Phelps was fired up with the possibilities. Soon enough, short-term actions were taken to move in the direction in which we wanted to go. Michael would stop playing lacrosse and baseball. He would go to a school where his teachers would support his swimming efforts. He would attend every practice every day. That's what the great ones do. Even though he was just a young boy and his everyday life really hadn't changed that much after my plan was revealed to him, Michael was now on a course that could take him somewhere special.

And all of us—Michael, his parents, his sisters, me—had that flame burning somewhere within us. We weren't just teaching Michael to swim an exceptional butterfly; we were building a world-record-breaking butterfly. We weren't just getting Michael to do push-ups and pull-ups; we were laying the foundation of fitness for an Olympic champion.

Simply put: The vision must inspire you. It should be exciting and emotional; it should speak to your heart as well as your mind. The mental picture of your achieving it should give you goosebumps. Yes, it can be far off, maybe a little vague. But what it can't be is tedious, routine, the same old.

RULE 1.7: YOUR VISION MUST ENGAGE YOU.

Now, you're asking, *What's the plan for achieving my vision and applying the everyday effort required?* Hold on. We'll get to that soon enough. First, let's get back to that meeting with my swimmers, the one that launched our Rio push.

From a shoebox-like office space I have adjacent to the meeting area, I could hear the swimmers joking and teasing one another. But, as soon as I opened my door and they saw me, the bantering came to a stop. Even Michael, the biggest star and the biggest kid in the room, knew enough to quiet down.

I had known some of these young men and women for years, others for only a short time. But everyone in that room knew one thing: When I walk through the door, the business day starts.

The day before, I had emailed each swimmer an outline of "the Game Plan" that would, in the best of all possible worlds, lead them to achieve their primary vision. To be clear, that vision was *not* to win gold in Rio; too many factors beyond their control could get in the way of achieving something so singular. No, our mission was simply to put them in the position to achieve such a possibility; to use the time between September 2013 and the first swimming event of the 2016 Olympics to prepare them to compete at the highest level—and, along the way, to teach them something about themselves that they might retain long after the Olympic torch had been extinguished.

My hope was to keep this meeting brief—thirty minutes tops. I would review the Game Plan, but mostly I would reinforce its intent. With the swimmers sitting there on foldout chairs, their lanky bodies slouched in the typical swimmer's pose, I stood before them and laid it out:

"I want each practice to be relevant. I want you to have a reason to be here. There is a culture of excellence here at the North Baltimore Aquatic Club, here at Meadowbrook. Some of you have been coming here for years, others for just a short time. Regardless, you know we're not about having fancy facilities or slick uniforms or working out on the techiest weight machines. No, this is simply a place for performing at the highest levels. Yes, in its essence this is a pool, but this place has its own culture. It's a combination of strategic thinking, planning, and total commitment to achieving one's goals with little regard for external conditions. It is all about who you are inside and how you choose to approach your life and your swimming."

I caught my breath, then went on.

"We will ask for more effort, more focus, more persistence, more toughness, more training, more creative thinking, more problem-solving, and more honesty than you've ever put forth. These are the hallmarks of champions. People, this is the first day of our preparation for Rio 2016. That's what this whole meeting is about. And these are the things that we believe in. These are the objectives. This is the Method we're going to follow."

I paused for a second and looked at the group. I tried to look each swimmer in the eye, to gauge each one's level of interest. Then I kept going. "Let's make it crystal clear what I expect, and if you don't want to buy into it, that's okay. You can leave right now. But if you're going to be here this is how we're going to do it." I stopped and looked into their faces again. Each swimmer was staring back at me. I knew I had them engaged, and I knew they realized why they were here. They'd come here for a reason.

They had a dream, and I was going to help them turn it into a reality.

3

RULE 2: ADOPT AN "ALL-IN!" ATTITUDE, NOT A "GET OUT!" ONE

Let me tell you one of my favorite Michael Phelps anecdotes. I like it for many reasons, including one in particular. See if you can figure it out. (By the way, with this retelling I've changed the name of one of the individuals in the story; you'll understand why in a second.)

A couple of months before the 2004 Summer Olympics in Athens, Michael and I went to a fund-raising dinner for a local Baltimore charity. During the event, we ran into the mother of one of Michael's teammates from Meadowbrook. Now, at the time Michael was all of eighteen years old, just a year out of high school and not accustomed to attending fancy dinners. Plus, in our immediate focus was the upcoming Olympic Trials, which would determine whether or not Michael made it to Athens. So on this night he was feeling a little edgy—setting the stage for nothing positive when Mrs. Know-it-all approached us and said,

"Michael, is it true? You're thinking of swimming the hundred-meter butterfly at the Trials? Why? You'll have no shot of winning that at the Olympics."

Oh, Mrs. Know-it-all, this isn't the time or place for such input. I could see Michael tense up as he prepped his comeback. But, just as he was about to volley a reply, I intercepted the moment and said, "Got to run, Mrs. Know-it-all. There's a buffet table calling us." Over dinner a few minutes later, Michael let loose on Mrs. Know-it-all.

"What does she know?" he groused.

I told him, "Let it go. She has no clue."

Fast-forward ten weeks, to the evening of August 20, and to the Athens Olympic Aquatic Centre. There's Michael, in a pool not far from the championship one, cooling down . . . from his *gold-medal* swim in the finals of the 100-meter butterfly. Yes, he won the event and in an Olympic-record time. Seconds after his victory, I had left the stands and rushed over to find him. He had been matched against the world-record holder, Ian Crocker, and he trailed Crocker until the very last stroke of the race. I wanted to know what he was thinking as he desperately tried to make up ground. I wanted to know what it was like to win his sixth gold medal in as many nights. Most of all, I wanted to know where we were going for dinner.

Turns out he had other things on his mind.

When he saw me, he called out, "Hey, Bob!"

Hmm. I didn't like the tone of his voice. He sounded edgy, and not like a kid pumped with post-race euphoria.

I bent down and got closer to the pool deck. "Yes?" I said with trepidation.

"Remember that fund-raiser we went to a couple of months ago?" he asked.

"Yessss . . ." I said, this time stringing out my reply. I couldn't tell where he was going.

"Remember how Mrs. Know-it-all told me I could never win the hundred-'fly and I shouldn't even enter it?" I nodded. A grin started to crease his face. "Well, what's up now, Mrs. Know-it-all?" And, with that, he turned away and eased down the pool, a kid with another gold medal and, seemingly, one less worry in his head.

As he moved farther away, I thought, So, that's what you're thinking about when you're racing for a gold medal? Some pesky lady back in Baltimore?

RULE 2.1: "ALL-IN" CAN TURN LONG SHOTS INTO LEGENDS.

People ask me all the time, "What makes Michael such a great swimmer?" They expect me to say his size, which features an eighty-inch wingspan that must come in handy when reaching for a swimming pool's wall. Or his double-jointed, size-14 feet, which some people suspect work like flippers. Or that he can eat fifty-seven chicken wings in an hour and still jump into a pool and plow through water without retching.

They want me to say he's Superman.

But then I tell them a story like the one with Mrs. Know-it-all and the answer becomes oh-so-obvious. What has made Michael the greatest Olympic champion of all time is something that each of us can bring to our vision pursuit: the right attitude. The kind of attitude that drives success. And by that I don't mean that Michael just loves to win. That's a given with an athlete who has accomplished what Michael has.

No, his attitude embraces something subtler.

Michael, you see, cannot stand to lose. Or to be told that he can't achieve something. Or to be seen by others as lagging. It is that attitude—I refer to it as the All-In Attitude—that has gotten him to four Olympics and, potentially, to a fifth. It has gotten him to the medal stand a record number of times. And it has gotten doubters like Mrs. Know-it-all to become believers.

Let me be clear: The right attitude, the All-In Attitude, can turn long shots into legends. The wrong attitude— the one people identify with complainers, slouchers, and corner-cutters—will have coaches, bosses, managers yelling "Get out!" at those who bring it to the task at hand. My plan for everyday excellence and long-term achievement works best with the All-In crowd, not the "Get out!" types.

In my ten-step Method having or developing the All-In Attitude is critical. In fact, it's essential. Unless you have the inclination to be a positive, an inspired, a "What-more-can-I-do?" participant, and unless that inclination is engaged throughout the process of achieving your vision, you won't completely enjoy success should you attain it.

RULE 2.2: SEEK TO ACHIEVE, NOT TO MEDAL.

Notice that I don't use the adjective "winning" to describe the right attitude. There's a reason for that, and it goes back to something I held off explaining in the previous chapter. Remember I said that my vision as a young coach was to develop record-breaking swimmers, not Olympic gold medalists. Here's why I make that distinction; it will help you see the value of the All-In Attitude.

In all my years of coaching Michael and other world-class swimmers, I have never made "to win an Olympic gold medal" their primary mission. I tell them, "Gold medals are out of your control. Another swimmer may simply be better than you on race day." But if they set their sights on breaking a record—at nailing the best time possible—then they can visualize something that's tangible, achievable, and within their control.

For a young athlete to see that distinction, he must have the proper outlook. An attitude that's geared toward achieving personal satisfaction and serving the needs of a team—and not toward simply gaining public recognition.

Now, don't get me wrong: I've enjoyed the star treatment that comes with being Michael's coach. Winning is fun, and it leads to terrific rewards. I've certainly gotten a kick out of appearing on NBC to talk about Michael after a gold-medal performance. And I was named head coach of the U.S. Olympic men's swimming team for the Rio Games in part, I'm sure, because of my success with Michael. And speaking of Michael: He doesn't make the cover of

Sports Illustrated a half-dozen times if all of his medals are silver.

But when Michael and I are alone and away from the cameras and the microphones, we talk about his finishing times, not his medal count. What motivates him is personal performance and excellence. Such focus is the product of bringing the proper attitude to his pursuits.

Let me show you how it can work.

RULE 2.3: TAKE THE "WHY NOT JUST TRY IT?" APPROACH.

We have a slogan at Meadowbrook that appears on our bulletin boards and on the T-shirts that our youngest swimmers wear to competitions: "Attitude. Action. Achievement." It's short and memorable and perfectly sums up what we think is necessary for success, in the pool and in life.

Notice what comes first? Attitude. You cannot achieve anything, I believe, unless you bring the right attitude to the pool, to the classroom, to the office—even to the family room.

As I've already pointed out, everyone can have a vision. Remember, all it takes is a little creative thinking, a little imagination. And we all know people who have expressed visions: *I want to switch careers. I want to eat healthier and lose thirty pounds. I want to be smarter about my finances and save toward a retirement home. I want to help my kids get the most out of their young lives.* We can all dream about things. We can see these things in our mind's eye and say, "Wow, wouldn't it be great . . . ?"

But what happens? All too often there is no follow-through.

We settle for the job we have, and the reliable paycheck that comes with it. We break down and stop at the fast-food restaurant instead of listening to our heads and getting home to a meal of salad and salmon. We decide to play thirty-six holes of golf instead of just eighteen, forgetting that the kids have a family-movie night planned.

I chalk up such failures to attitude. As I see it, if your attitude is uninspired, lagging, unequal to your vision, then nothing great will be achieved.

But if the attitude is reversed, well, then exceptional things can happen.

Let my Grandmother Helen show you what I mean.

Growing up on the outskirts of Columbia, South Carolina, I devoted most of my time to living a typical suburban life: school, football, band, and then lots of swimming once I discovered the sport at the age of eleven. But, come summer, I would spend many days with my mom's parents out on their hundred-acre farm in the tiny town of Clover, South Carolina (population: 5,399). It's where Mom and her six siblings were raised by their taciturn father, Tom, and his spitfire wife, Helen. As a kid, I longed for those days on the farm with Paw and Maw, not just because I actually grew to love the work of cleaning barns and picking corn but also because I could hang out with Maw Helen and listen to her stories, like the following one.

She once told me that when she turned fifty-five, and the

last of her kids was grown and out of the house, she decided to pursue a dream she had held on to for thirty years: to get a college degree. "Why do you need to do that?" Paw would ask. Maw didn't answer. She had this *Why not just try it?* way about her. So, while friends and family members her age were preparing to retire or slow down, she set off to get her college degree.

In my travels around the world, I've met some of the most famous and successful people of our day—from the British prime minister Tony Blair to the heavyweight champion Muhammad Ali. But when people ask me who my hero is I tell them Maw Helen. She taught me the power of the *Why not just try it?* approach to life—and it has served me (and many others) very well.

RULE 2.4: MOVE FORWARD WITH POSITIVE ENERGY.

Maw and I spent quality time together. Michael and I spend quality *and* quantity time together. Over the past two decades, we've developed a multifaceted relationship: coach/athlete, business partners, friends. But, as much as we're around each other, I still sometimes see him as the kid who used to drive the lifeguards crazy by instigating towel fights with his little buddies in the Meadowbrook locker room.

With that picture in mind, I don't often think of him as being, well, very profound.

But a few years back he was quoted as saying the

following: "You can't put a limit on anything. The more you dream, the farther you get." The quote gets tweeted quite often, and for good reason.

Michael is speaking about moving forward, and to do so you need positive energy.

Here's an example of someone who brings such energy to his daily effort. Meet Tom Luchsinger. Around Meadowbrook, we called Tom Mr. Perfect, but that wasn't because of his record in swim meets. In fact, ever since he turned professional, after completing an outstanding college career at North Carolina, Tom has struggled in competitions. Throughout his first year with me, we worked to determine what was holding him back, with the hope that, come the Olympic Trials in June 2016, he'd be back in sync.

But, even though race days often proved frustrating, Tom didn't let the results affect his everyday performance. You see, he has this upbeat personality that makes everyone around him feel better, even when they know they face a long day ahead in the pool. Swimming can be a tedious sport. Practices are year-round, and often take place before the sun comes up. During Tom's first year with me, Baltimore suffered through one of its coldest, snowiest winters in decades. Many mornings I would look out my window and not want to go to practice—and I didn't have to get into the water. Every morning, though, Tom was there, always on time. He'd also be the one picking up teammates when their cars wouldn't start. He remembered birthdays, too—and sent tweets so that everyone else did as well.

You see? Mr. Perfect.

We were lucky to have Tom in our club. He had the All-In Attitude, and because of that the NBAC team—coaches, swimmers, support staff—worked collectively to sharpen him for the Olympic Trials run.

RULE 2.5: DO YOURSELF A FAVOR AND AVOID NEGATIVE ENTHUSIASM.

I admit it: I was lucky that Tom Luchsinger sought me out as his coach. I came to know of his work ethic and dedication to the little things during the course of our training sessions. But sometimes you can't afford to "discover" whether or not someone has the right attitude. You need to determine if that quality is there before you bring him into your company or onto your team.

So, you're asking, how can you tell if a person has the *attitude*, and not just "attitude"? Good question. The answer is more difficult to pin down.

As I've learned, spotting the All-In Attitude comes with trial and error, and after all these years I can't guarantee that I'll be perfectly on target when selecting a swimmer or an employee who is right for my program. What I do know is that I need to make All-In a priority during my search; otherwise, my team and I will suffer. So what I do is play detective, looking for clues that will indicate whether or not individuals are suited for my team—and whether or not I'm suited to train them.

When Michael was eleven or so, he left plenty of clues. I used to watch him play a game with his friends called Wall Ball. They would dart back and forth against a long wall that we had at Meadowbrook, hoping not to get beaned by a tennis ball. Michael would dodge, leap, duck . . . whatever was necessary to avoid getting clocked. More times than not, he succeeded.

At that point he was not an Olympic champion, but via Wall Ball Michael sure provided clues of his competitive nature.

Clues. You have to look for them, because whether you're the manager of employees or a coach of athletes, one of your primary tasks is to bring new personnel into an organization or onto a team. To stay competitive, you have to restock the talent pool. When hiring, you'll often look first at a résumé—in my opinion, one of the most ineffective recruitment tools in play. For sure, a résumé lists a person's achievements and successes. But if you've been in the managing/coaching business long enough, you know that a résumé tells only part of a person's story. It rarely says how the person achieved these results. How she reacted when failure came along. How he helped others on deadline nights. How much fun she was to work with, or how much cynicism he brought to Monday-morning meetings.

Ultimately, you want to know if your potential hire has

the comportment, the work ethic, the desire, the goods to fit in with your group. You want to know what approach—yes, what attitude—this person will bring to the job.

In my case, I want to know what kind of enthusiasm this person will bring, positive or negative. You're asking yourself, *Negative enthusiasm? Is there such a thing?* I know, it sounds like an oxymoron. What I mean, though, is that some people fail to exude passion for a project or a vision. They say they want to accomplish something, but their actions don't reflect that desire. In a sense, they're negating any enthusiasm they might have.

So when hiring for my staff or when signing up a new swimmer, I look for signs of both "positive" and "negative" enthusiasm. It takes effort, some sleuthing skills, but the payoff is tremendous. For instance, in 2011, just before the London Olympics, I began searching for a new assistant coach, someone who I thought might someday take over for me when my coaching days were over. Obviously, an important hire.

I interviewed several coaches, including Erik Posegay, a relatively young coach (he was only thirty-one at the time) who came highly recommended. When I first met Erik, I have to say I was a bit unimpressed. I asked him to tell me a little about himself, something I wouldn't find on his résumé. He seemed mild, low-key . . . yes, not too inspiring. I thought, *This guy is going to replace me, Bob "Big Mouth" Bowman?* I had all but given up on the interview when I asked Erik to talk about some of his swimmers and what training methods he found worked. Suddenly, Erik's personality shifted. His eyes brightened, and so did our conversation. He began sharing stories of his swimmers' successes, including that of a high schooler who had just set a national record. He talked about how "we did it," not how "I did it." He became effusive, enthusiastic.

I had uncovered what engaged him: getting young athletes to develop and improve under his watch.

Erik had what I was looking for: coaching skills, management skills and, most important, positive enthusiasm. Days later, he became my new assistant coach.

RULE 2.6: BE SURE TO SHOW OFF YOUR ALL-IN APPROACH.

Playing detective is central to uncovering attitude. Learn to play it well. When interviewing a job candidate, for instance, ask questions that can decipher how much preparation she did for a meeting. Are her answers substantive and studied—or simply rote? Likewise, take note of the questions she asks you; ideally, the candidate should be incisive, not predictable. She should challenge you. On a second interview, gauge both the depth and the tenor of her answers. There should be energy in her voice, some confidence and assuredness. At this point, you should feel as if you're having a conversation, not an interrogation. Your attitudes are aligning. You're seeing this person's vision, and hearing her enthusiasm.

As you can see, I'm big on positive enthusiasm. A coach's job is to help turn someone's vision into a reality. That's what I do. But, before I can help someone, she must convince me that she truly wants to achieve. Her attitude, and how she manifests it, is often the best indicator.

Take Yannick Agnel as proof.

In the spring of 2013, I had brought my swimmers to Colorado Springs and to the United States Olympic Committee training center for several weeks of high-altitude workouts. Over the years I've learned that training in the thin Rocky Mountain air can make my crew especially strong as we head into racing season. One afternoon during that trip, I was having lunch with Keenan Robinson, my team's longtime strength, conditioning, and athletic trainer. As I'm inclined to do, I kept checking my iPhone while we ate. At one point, I received a direct message via Twitter.

I'd like to come swim with you, it read.

Come again? I thought. Talk about a strange message. Then I looked up to note the sender—and immediately thought someone was playing a joke on me.

Yannick Agnel was France's premier swimmer. At the London Games the previous summer, he led a relay team that upset the U.S. team, a foursome that included Michael. It was one of two gold medals Yannick won during the Games. (He also picked up a silver.) Everyone in the sport knew that he had the potential to do even bigger things, what with his youth (he was in his early twenties) and his build. At six feet eight, he looked down at Michael.

I looked at Keenan. "There's no way this is *that* Yannick," I said. "Why would he want to leave France to come swim in Baltimore?" I paused for a second. "If this guy really wants to talk to me, he can email me."

Which is exactly what he did seconds later. "I'd really like to talk to you," Yannick's email began.

Admittedly, I was still skeptical but now also curious. Cryptically, I emailed this Yannick character back, telling him that I would be in Colorado just through Saturday and then I had several trips planned. I wouldn't be returning to Baltimore for a few weeks. "Call me when I'm back home," I wrote, then hit Send and looked over at Keenan.

"That should end the conversation," I said.

Minutes later . . . *buzz.*

"Can I come meet you in Colorado Springs on Saturday?" the reply email read. I didn't have much of a response except, "It's up to you."

Three days later, a brown-haired giant walked into the aquatic center. With a gentle French accent he said, "Hello, I am Yannick Agnel."

His actions (getting on a plane on short notice, flying 5,300 miles to meet a stranger) and his explanation ("I want to become an even better swimmer") demonstrated his enthusiasm not only for what I might be able to do for him but also for the vision he held of himself. He had something that he wanted to accomplish.

I shook his hand and said, "Welcome to our team." Yannick smiled and said, *"Très bien!"* And we both laughed.

That summer, he won two golds at the World Championships.

RULE 2.7: WHEN YOU GO OFF COURSE, READJUST YOUR APPROACH.

Reality check: I know that I've spent a good deal of time discussing the value of a positive, engaged attitude toward achieving your vision. Well, I also know that none of us can always be upbeat, inspired, All-In all of the time. Yes, even Tom Luchsinger will acknowledge that there are moments when frustration can produce pessimism. And I can certainly cite days when Michael would drive me crazy with a lackadaisical demeanor.

In fact, for the better part of the run-up to the London Games, Michael's attitude—or altered attitude—became a wedge that almost ruined our relationship. This development originated after his celebrated achievement in Beijing, where he had won his eight medals and had broken Mark Spitz's record. He had fulfilled a dream, and with it came the accolades—more magazine covers, TV appearances, and sponsorship deals. Suddenly, he had interests beyond swimming the length of a pool.

I understood that he had these new ventures, and I also knew that he needed time to grow beyond the confines of the swimming world. He was still a young man, for God's sake. But I also knew that he had made a commitment to swim in the London Olympics, and if he didn't get his act together—make it to more practices, race sharper in meets, give more respect to his coach—a huge embarrassment was in the offing for him.

Simply put, we needed to get his edge, his All-In Attitude, back.

And we did, but it required a lot of "Get out!" shouting matches between the two of us, as well as a number of quiet conversations in which we diplomatically reset our vision for London—and for how we would get there. I kept stressing to him that pure physical talent wouldn't get him ready to compete. He needed to sharpen his focus, and soon. I didn't bring up Mrs. Know-it-all, but her presence loomed. If he didn't snap his attitude back into drive, he faced defeat in London, and being embarrassed on worldwide television in the process. I didn't mention winning medals, either. I spoke of losing face.

As I said earlier, losing motivates Michael more than winning.

The pushing and prodding finally took. On July 5, one month before the Games began, Michael showed up for a 7 A.M. practice; from that point on, he never missed another workout or was late for one during the run-up to the Games. The result? In London he won four more golds. Excellent results, or so most of America and the world thought. But Michael and I both knew how much better they could have been had he engaged his All-In Attitude sooner.

As a coach, I know that part of my job is to get my people excited about the prospects that lie ahead of them. Unfortunately, I have also learned that sometimes I cannot turn a "Get out!" attitude into an All-In one. With Michael, I eventually succeeded. But over the years I've applied the same tactics I used with Michael—some browbeating, some hand-holding—to try and push people to the next level, and they didn't work. When that happens, I momentarily feel like a failure; I didn't get that person to the dream place he sought. But I also know that, ultimately, it comes down to the person deciding whether he wants All-In or "Get out!"

RULE 2.8: ALL-IN BRINGS OUT ALL THE POSSIBILITIES.

Let me tell you something: It is so much fun when someone brings All-In to the job. Jessica Long is proof of that.

When she decided to join my team, Jessica had obviously known the joy of climbing a medal podium. At the London Games, she stood atop it five times. She could have been very satisfied with her résumé, and what she had proved already. But she came to me seeking new limits, and to educate others about possibilities.

As it turned out, she taught her new coach a few things as well.

I have to admit, I got the willies when Jessica first started coming to practice. I would walk the pool deck while the swimmers warmed up, and then suddenly I'd see a pair of legs just lying on the ground. I'm used to seeing goggles, kick boards, and suntan lotion around the deck, not prosthetics. It took me a while to get comfortable with the sight. I also worried about working Jessica too hard. I wondered if she could handle the types of workouts I was preparing for the likes of Michael, Yannick, and Allison.

With one of my drills, I'm constantly encouraging the swimmers to use their legs more. I'll bark, "Kick . . . harder! Work . . . the . . . legs! Use . . . your . . . legs!" One day, I noticed Jessica just moments after I had started yelling, "Use your legs!" I raced to the other end of the pool to apologize. "Jessica, forgive me. I uh, I uh . . ." She stopped me. "Bob, look, I get it. You don't have to apologize. These guys have legs. They should use them. Me? I'll do what I can." She shoved off the wall and raced to catch up to her teammates.

As a coach—especially one with a big mouth—that's the attitude you want your athletes to have.

Not long after that practice, Jessica was sitting at a picnic table, talking about her strokes and what she needed to work on and about making the Olympic Trials. She admitted that hitting the qualifying times would be difficult, especially given her physical challenges. But then, almost without thinking, she said, "A quote I live by is: 'The only disability in life is a negative attitude.'" She stopped for a second, and smiled. "I really believe that," she added, "especially with not having my legs."

Now, that's what I mean by All-In.

4

RULE 3: TAKE RISKS—AND THEN ENJOY THE REWARDS

On April 23, 2014, about eight months into his return to the pool, Michael sat before the media in Mesa, Arizona. The next day he would be swimming in his first meet since the August 2012 London Olympics, a span of 628 days. Back then he had told the press, and the world, that his career was over. In the time that had passed, no one suspected that anything had changed. Few in the media even knew that Michael had been working out since early September at Meadowbrook; he had told only his closest confidants about his plans to shoot for a spot on the U.S. Olympic team in Rio. And he had no intention of making his news public today.

The questions came fast, but MP was ready for each one.

REPORTER 1: Why are you racing again, Michael?

MP: *I just missed being back in the water.*

REPORTER 2: What's your plan right now?

MP: *I'm really just trying to see how much weight I can lose, see what kind of shape I can get into, and see what happens from there.*

REPORTER 3: What are your long-term plans?

MP: *I just enjoy being in the pool. Just being able to get back in that mentality of competition. That's the one thing I really loved about swimming the most.*

I sat beside him, microphones positioned on the table in front of us. I chuckled under my breath at some of his answers, especially the one about his weight. During his time away from the pool and during his golf travels, he had bulked up from a London weight of 185 pounds to one of 225 pounds. The recent workouts had gotten him under 200, but not that much under. At one point during the press conference I had started to tell a reporter about his conditioning—"When he came back, he was so out of shape." Then Michael cut in.

"Sugarcoat it, Bob," he said with a half smile.

Laughter filled the press tent. I smirked and then went on. "It took a while to get to a point where he could swim in public. It is a process."

The press conference was due to last about fifteen minutes, and throughout most of it Michael handled the questions with relative ease. He had been around reporters for so long—he did his first interview, probably, when he was twelve—that he knew just how much information and insight to hand out. He gave answers that were, for sure, a bit tepid, but answers all the same. In fact, it seemed that with every question asked he found a way to sneak in a variation on the "fun" theme: *"I'm just having fun." "It's been fun so far." "I'm just having fun with my new teammates."*

And then came the question that threatened to trip him up.

"Michael, if you do come back and you do make it to Rio," a reporter began, "do you worry that you might be risking your legacy if things don't turn out well?"

Michael chuckled a little. So did I. Up to this point in his return, we hadn't given much thought to "risking his legacy." He looked over at me before answering. I just raised my eyebrow, as if to say, "You're on your own with this one, friend."

He waited a second, rolling his tongue under his lower lip. Finally, and with emphasis, he said, "I'm doing this for me. I'm doing this because I enjoy being in the pool and I enjoy the sport of swimming. I am looking forward to wherever this road takes me."

The reporters scribbled the quotes into their notebooks. Michael took a swig of water. And I thought, Well done, MP.

In my world and in his world, we knew what came with taking risks—and with not taking them. His answer connected to a central principle of the Method: You grow by taking chances, and you reach your dreams by taking them, too. In a sense, risks provide the fuel needed to get on the road to, as Michael put it, *wherever* you want to go.

RULE 3.1: LIFE GETS LIVELIER BY TAKING A RISK NOW AND THEN.

Many psychologists will tell you that, once people hit a level of comfort, they tend to get complacent. They're happy. They're satisfied.

In my opinion, they're also on the road to boredom and inertia.

I live by the maxim that unless I take a chance—unless I push the risk meter—I'm going to stagnate, and that's not good for me, the people who work for me, or those who swim for me.

Let me give you a few examples of the risks I've taken: I invested in a seventy-eight-year-old swimming facility just when the last great recession took hold. I put thousands of dollars into the horse-racing business, a sport whose best days (from a spectator and a betting perspective) were years ago. I uprooted myself at the age of fifty—a time when many people start thinking of retirement—and moved to Arizona to try and revive a down-and-out swim program. I took a chance on a swimmer named Phelps, who could just as easily have burned out on the sport as turn into the greatest Olympic athlete ever. With these investments, I gambled. And over the course of time they've given me plenty of heartaches and headaches. But they've also been infinitely rewarding, both financially and emotionally.

Best of all, each risk I've taken has subsequently prepared me to take more risks—a habit that more easily lets me turn visions into reality.

I've talked about the need to have a vision. I've stressed the value of displaying the proper attitude. Now I'm going to suggest one more item to have in your pursuit of everyday excellence and long-term dreams: a tolerance for taking risks.

To my mind, the magnitude of an achievement will be limited by your aversion to risk. Building up your risk tolerance is like building up your fitness. You have to start small, and you have to go through some pain, but once you get the feel for risk's ebbs and flows, its highs and lows, you learn to appreciate it. I understand that there can be negative consequences to risk-taking—as you'll see in the pages to come, my bank account took a hit when I decided to invest in an aquatic center. But, the way I view it, I'm going to learn plenty from the failures that often come with risk-taking. Somehow, I will gain, either now or down the road.

Understand something: I don't come to my elevated level of risk tolerance naturally. God bless my dad, Lonnie, and my mom, Sylvia. At this point they are both in their seventies, and they are both incredibly secure and happy with the lives they've lived and the lifestyles they've chosen. But they would be the first to admit that they've shied away from taking many chances. For instance, each held the same job for more than thirty years, and in their eyes everything worked out fine. Their steady salaries got my sister, Donna, and me through college and paid off the mortgage on their house in Columbia. Along the way, Dad even learned to play a pretty good game of golf.

Still, I can't help thinking that their lives may be even more fulfilled had they taken more risks. For instance, Mom and Dad still live in the house I grew up in. For years I've been begging them to move out of the neighborhood, because it's not as safe as it once was. But Dad can't even think about it. He says he's too old to buy a new place and start paying a new mortgage. He would rather just make sure the money he has saved goes to Donna and me. I keep telling him, "Don't save it for us! We're okay!" He won't listen.

That kind of thinking serves him well; it's just not my kind of thinking. I take more after Maw Helen. When I made my first investment in a thoroughbred racehorse in 1996, one of the first people I told was Maw. "That's my boy," she said, not caring that, at thirty-two, I was hardly a boy anymore. In the time that has passed, I've invested with Michael in several more horses. We tend to name them after moments from our past. Water Cube, for instance, got his moniker from the nickname of the Beijing National Aquatics Center, the site of MP's eight gold medals. Owning a horse is an expensive and, yes, risky proposition. So far, my stable hasn't produced many stakes winners, but it has produced loads of fun and given me a chance to dream about Triple Crowns, not just about gold medals.

The horses also prompt me to keep looking for something new to try, a little gamble to take. I believe that to move closer to fulfilling your vision and your overall personal promise, you need to be open to the occasional risk.

I only have to look to one of my favorite swimmers to be reminded of the potential payoff when you do.

And I'm not talking about Michael Phelps this time.

RULE 3.2: ALL-IN ATTITUDES OFTEN MAKE FOR VERY GOOD GAMBLES.

In the winter of 2011, a young swimmer decided to move from Pennsylvania to Baltimore to swim for the development program at NBAC. If you do well in the junior division, you have a shot at moving up to our élite group. In the case of this swimmer, I couldn't help noticing her when she was in the water, though it wasn't because she was exceptionally fast compared to the other fifteen-year-olds we had. In fact, she had a ways to go to keep up with them.

No, what distinguished Cierra Runge was her size. She was already six feet three (and on her way to an eventual six feet four).

Cierra definitely had talent, but she had never trained the ultra-intensive way we do at Meadowbrook, and it showed. When competitions came, she tended to let the pressure of the moment get to her. In races in which she should have placed, she finished out of contention. For her to move to the next level, I knew that we would need to push her more. My assistants, Erik and Keenan, worked with her. They came up with training plans that, on paper, seemed ideally suited to Cierra. But all their planning and all the extra attention did little—except make Erik and Keenan so frustrated that they suggested that Cierra might not be right for our program.

I could have listened to the two of them and accepted their verdict. We have a large program; upwards of 220 kids train at Meadowbrook. I don't guarantee that everyone who joins us will become an Olympian, and I don't have enough coaches and trainers on staff to give each swimmer special treatment. Still, there was something about this young girl . . . Cierra was such a good-natured kid, with an All-In Attitude. Those attributes made her a risk worth the investment of some extra time and TLC.

"Guys, I appreciate the standards you're trying to maintain," I told Erik and Keenan, "but you've got to remember our job is not to keep the perfect ones and get rid of the imperfect ones. It's to try to have everybody move toward his or her potential. Otherwise, one day there's not going to be anybody left." I paused for a moment. "And Cierra has potential. Let's just work with her, okay?"

Right there, I was taking another risk. I risked losing my two coaches. I had hired them because I knew they were good at evaluating talent and plotting workouts based on their assessments. I didn't want them to lose confidence in themselves or feel that they couldn't confide in me when concerns arose.

For the next year, my bet on Cierra looked like a 50–1 shot at Pimlico Race Course. Cierra continued to struggle in big meets. At the 2012 Olympic Trials, she finished well out of contention in the events she swam.

Now I was getting frustrated, but not so much that I wasn't willing to consider one more risky move.

Throughout her competitive career, Cierra had primarily been a sprinter. Nothing surprising there. Swimming tradition held that tall kids made for good sprinters. But the way she swam, with long, languid strokes versus the rapid, pulverizing ones of a sprinter, got me thinking: Maybe she's better suited to longer distances. So one day in early 2013, I called Cierra over before practice. "You're training in the distance group today," I told her. Her face twisted. I tried not to notice. "I don't care if you like it or not. We're going to do something different and we'll see what happens."

And what happened? She became a bubbling star. She took to the distance races—the 400 meters, the 800 meters—as if Intel had programmed her for them. Soon colleges around the country came calling; she became one of the most highly recruited high-school swimmers in years. Eventually, she chose Cal Berkeley, and in her freshman year she set a collegiate record in the 500-yard freestyle while helping to lead the Bears to a national championship. In the process, she established herself as a podium contender in Rio.

Perhaps more important than the records and the accolades, Cierra has realized the potential she always had. But it took a risk—on my part and, certainly, on hers.

Risk comes in many forms, and yet in whatever flavor it appears you need to project the value of the possible reward. Sometimes the payoff isn't worth the potential for loss. In Cierra's case, I had much to lose. As I pointed out, I had to consider whether Erik and Keenan would take my pushback as an affront to their own abilities. And I had to consider whether other swimmers might be put off by the added attention I was giving to Cierra. But I hold to the following principle: When dealing with people—especially young people who are still in the early part of their careers—you don't want to miss the chance to help them grow by giving up on them too soon. Their unrealized potential is worth all the added effort you can make to get their dreams a little closer to reality.

RULE 3.3: TAKING A RISK CAN BRING UNEXPECTED GROWTH.

As a coach of Olympic-caliber athletes, I often get judged by the number of medals my swimmers earn or the world records they break. Yes, I'm fine with that; such measuring sticks have always been a part of my profession. And, yes, I will drive my athletes endlessly in order to have them ready to compete in peak condition. Anyone who stops by one of my practices will hear me bellowing, "You gotta push this last one harder!" or, "This last fifty *MUST* be your fastest one!" long before they hear, "Well done, everybody."

But I also know that my athletes and my employees perform better when they're not so consumed by developing their professional skills that they fail to enhance their personal lives. I want them to grow as people while they're developing into champions. That means they have to test themselves beyond the confines of a 50-meter pool.

In any endeavor, the more well rounded you are the better prepared you'll be to handle the highs and lows that come with a particular specialty. One thing that makes Yannick Agnel fun to coach is his assorted interests out of the pool. From his European sensibilities to his taste in literature and music, Yannick has positioned himself nicely. He can quickly forget about a bad day of practice by diving into the latest novel he's reading, a little fuel for a strong comeback the next day.

That said, if too many issues are assaulting one's inner peace, performance is bound to suffer. I often hear of people who have consistently been high performers—top-selling salespeople, award-winning schoolteachers, Hall of Fame–caliber football players—until they suddenly lose their edge. As it turns out, the affected have not endured a talent drain; rather, something in their personal world has gone awry and caused a performance breakdown. A lot of times, I've found, a person doesn't get fully back on track until he opens up to someone about his troubles.

I know what you're thinking: Sharing personal struggles isn't easy. You tell a boss that something is bugging you and you might not get the next big assignment that comes along.

Yes, revelation can be risky business—as Jessica Long will tell you, too.

The thing is, she'll also tell you the possibilities that can come with it.

I've mentioned Jessica a couple of times already, and each time it has been in the context of "Jessica the swimmer." Now I want you to know a little bit about "Jessica the person"—a person willing to take risks both in and out of the water.

Obviously, Jessica took a gamble in moving to Baltimore from Colorado Springs, where she had trained for years, training that had culminated in an incredible medal haul. With her physical challenges, she had to work extra hard now to keep up with her new teammates. Some days I would see the stress on her face as she walked away from the pool after a practice, her usual smile replaced by a look of consternation. I could understand: She was a competitive athlete used to success, and these workouts were testing her limits.

One day, though, I got the sense that something more than achy muscles was weighing her down. I approached her and said, "Jessica, is everything okay?"

She paused before saying anything, and then confessed, "Bob, I hope you don't mind, but I'm going to need to take a couple of weeks off from training."

To be honest, it wasn't the news I wanted to hear. I had worked pretty hard to get her into NBAC shape. With two weeks away from the pool, a good deal of fitness might disappear. But before I could voice any displeasure she jumped in. "Listen, I'm going over to Russia to meet my parents. My biological parents. I'm sorry I'll miss some practices, but I've got to do this."

With that piece of information, what could I say except "Of course, go. I totally understand. Let me know what I can do for you."

Imagine for a second: You are born in Siberia with severe physical disabilities and then you're put up for adoption. You get a break, though. An American couple adopts you before you're even a year old and then brings you to live in suburban America. Good schools. Plenty of activities. Devoted parents and fun siblings. You accept your physical challenges—you have to walk practically on your knees when you're not wearing your prosthetics—and through lots of hard work you become an American champion, a multigold medalist at the Paralympics. And you have more dreams: to model, to be on TV, to write a memoir.

Everything seems perfect. A story with a happy ending. Just leave it as is, right?

In the back of your mind, though, you wonder, Where did I come from? It's a thought few kids in suburban America ever need to address.

Jessica did, but it wasn't until after the 2012 Paralympics that she decided to act on it.

Following the Games, and with all the notoriety that came via her performance, Jessica received word about her biological parents. It turned out that her mother was just sixteen when she gave birth. Knowing that she might not be suited to care for a child with Jessica's disabilities, she and the father put their baby up for adoption. Later, the mother and father married and had three more children.

Such knowledge might be enough to satisfy some people's curiosity. But not Jessica's. She wanted to know more about who she was and where she came from. So she took a risk.

Just before the 2014 Winter Olympics in Sochi, Jessica flew to Moscow and then took an eighteen-hour train ride to a town in Siberia—where she met her parents and a new set of siblings. She found missing pieces to her world, and they brought more peace to her life.

NBC later told the story of her reunion during the Winter Olympics. Yes, hard-ass Bob Bowman cried when he watched. I cried because I could see again that beautiful smile that I had gotten to know so well. And I cried because I knew that what she did had required a lot of courage. She took a risk different from many others. A career wasn't at stake, nor was a personal fortune.

No, a person's emotional self was at play.

When Jessica returned to the States, she was not in the same condition as when she'd left. She was in *better* shape, at least mentally. In the months that followed, she would break a world record that she had set three years earlier. Sure, I'd like to think the Method had something to do with her performance. I know, though, that a gutsy decision to travel "home" played a very big part.

I want my athletes to push themselves intellectually, culturally, and socially beyond the limits of the pool—and I challenge friends (and even myself) to do the same. Sure, that may not mean enduring a test like the one Jessica faced. Still, if we don't feel good about our personal selves, if something is playing with our mind-set, we won't have the clarity to pursue our visions.

To get needed balance, sometimes a risk comes in handy.

RULE 3.4: TO BECOME RISK-TOLERANT, YOU NEED TO FACE UP TO UNCERTAINTY.

Okay, I've shown you a couple of examples of the rewards that come with risk-taking. *Great*, you're saying, *but how do you turn a wallflower into a daredevil?*

Yes, I know the predicament. Perhaps you're someone who wants to try a new career track, but you look at your lucrative salary and your age ("Holy cow! I'm *that* old!") and all you can say is: "As much as I want to change things up, it isn't happening. I'm too comfortable." Or maybe you're longing for a new setting—you want to move out to the Wild West after a lifetime on the urban East Coast—but you're afraid of what you'll have to give up: longtime friends, favorite restaurants, a safe routine.

Sometimes the security of our lives keeps us from living life. But if you want to take that "next step" toward the dream you're after, you'll need to become a bit riskier.

Maybe it's because I'm a swim coach, but I believe the trick to raising risk tolerance is a lot like learning how to swim. Let me explain: Whether you're a toddler or a senior citizen, the water can be pretty intimidating if you've never learned to swim. You see the ocean or a pool and you wonder, What will happen if I actually go under? Will I come back up? But once you put a toe in—as well as take a few lessons—the worries subside. Doggy paddle turns into consistent, clean strokes, bobbing makes room for practiced breathing techniques, and the fun of being around water replaces most fears.

Risk-taking is a scary proposition, but I maintain that a gradual yet consistent attempt at overcoming fear pays off. Yes, old dogs can learn new tricks. Old swimmers can, too. Just ask Ous Mellouli.

Okay, in people terms Ous is hardly old. He'll be thirty-two at the time of the next Olympics. But among the crew on our Dream Team Ous easily outdistanced most of the other swimmers. Still, the native of Tunisia shows few signs of slowing down, and his vision is to get to one more Olympics before retirement. Already, he has been to two Games. In Beijing he won the 1,500 meters; four years later, he went even longer and won the 10,000-meter open water swim. I was thrilled when he decided to spend time training with our team after years of working with one of the finest coaches in the sport, Dave Salo, at the University of Southern California. But Ous presented me with a challenge: He told me that he had thoughts of training for the 400-meter individual medley, a new event in his repertoire.

When he started working out with me, I noticed that he did something totally unconventional. These days, most élite swimmers do a flip turn at the end of their backstroke leg (the second of four strokes in the individual medley). But Ous learned the event at a time when swimmers did an open turn—you just touched the wall and turned around. A perfectly fine maneuver, except that it will slow you down.

Seeing him do the old-fashioned approach a few times, I finally asked, "Ous, what's up with the touch? Where's your flip turn?"

"Sorry, Coach, I never learned it," he said. "I'm afraid if I did it in a race I'd get hurt or get disqualified."

"Ous, you're giving away seconds and maybe victories with the turn you're using. We got to get you over that fear."

Here's what we did: I tried to reduce his anxiety by simplifying the process. Instead of having him practice the turn by going up to the wall, I told him to work in the middle of the pool, simulating the turn there, where he wouldn't have to worry about clocking the wall. We did this for several days. Kids half Ous's age watched from the pool deck and wondered what the old men were up to.

In some respects, it was a tedious process: an Olympian needing such coddling to overcome trepidation. But the more we practiced, and the more we practiced closer and closer to the wall, the more I saw the reward. Not only was Ous getting more comfortable with the turn; he was upping his willingness to take on greater risk.

Ous, I'm sure, will get his turn figured out in time for Rio. A measured approach will do that, whether you want to improve technique in the water or change careers. Let's consider the latter for a second. Should a person just bag her current job in order to pursue a new track? Of course not—unless she also has a nice trust fund in place. But what she can do is take small steps to see if the job she seeks really suits her long-range plan. For instance, if she has been in accounting all her life but now suddenly has an interest in Web development, she should take a programming class at night at a local college. Or she should invite one of her company's programmers out to lunch and grill him for insights.

Ultimately, she needs to do some research and take some preliminary steps; that will build up her confidence. And, as my swimmers can attest, confidence comes in handy when you're facing a new challenge.

RULE 3.5: CHANGE YOUR BEHAVIOR. IT WILL CHANGE HOW YOU LOOK AT YOURSELF.

Besides the small-step approach, I have another route to take when you're looking to become more risk-tolerant, and it starts with examining the mental picture you have of yourself.

All of us have what I call a comfort zone, a sense of who we are, where we've been, and what we're about. From this zone, people gain an awareness of what they do well, where they lag, and what they value. They also develop beliefs about themselves that reinforce their mental picture. Consulting with a number of sport psychologists who have worked with my athletes, I have come to believe that to change behavior—to become more risk-tolerant if you're predominantly risk-averse, for instance—you need to change that mental picture.

I'll use an example from my own life to show you what I mean. As a kid, I was petrified of roller coasters. I remember going to amusement parks with my buddies, and when they charged off to ride those metal monsters I hung back with the staid bumper cars. But, just after I graduated from college, while on a trip to Kings Island amusement park outside Cincinnati with a friend and his son, I finally decided to confront my fear. This kid was a certified roller-coaster geek, and as we drove to the park he talked up the thrill of riding Kings Island's famed coaster, the Vortex. "Mr. Bowman, you'll go on it with me, right?" he kept asking. I avoided answering him. As we drew closer and closer to the park's entrance, though, I visualized the scene:

> **ME:** *With the Vortex looming before us, my face turns whiter than the clouds.*
>
> **THE KID:** *"You're coming on, Mr. Bowman, right?" he goads me. "Don't to be afraid. If I can do it, you can."*

The thing is, the more I saw that picture, amazingly, the more at ease I became. That's because I also began visualizing a scene where I was getting off the beast with all my appendages attached and with a big laugh roaring up from the depths of my chest.

That day, I went on a roller coaster for the first time. You know what? I loved it. And, ever since, whenever I'm in the vicinity of a coaster I've never tried, I rush right to it, reveling in the chance to check one more off my coaster bucket list.

Now, in that case I overcame my fear in a matter of minutes. Oftentimes, the process takes longer, but the results are the same: A mountain, a monster—a *fear* is defeated because you have visualized the possibilities that taking a risk might produce.

Over the years, we've had a number of swimmers who look like Olympic gold medalists in practice. Come race day, though, they turn into jellyfish minus the sting. Rather than trust their ability and all the work they've put in, they fall back on a mental picture they have of themselves: They see a good, but not great, swimmer. They see competition that has previously beaten them. They succumb to a proven reality rather than risk all their energy and talent toward a potential breakthrough. As a result, they fail to put their best effort forward.

When I recognize this behavior, I tell the swimmer that he needs to visualize what might happen if he risks replacing the worn picture with a revamped one. "Change your mental picture and try going after a new, improved reality," I say.

Again, I'm not suggesting that this is an easy task. What I am saying is that, practiced regularly, such visualization can prove effective. I've used it so much, and to such advantage, that I now have Michael telling his teammates how it can work. At the 2013 USA National Championships, one of my most decorated swimmers, Allison Schmitt, had a disastrous meet. You'll recall that a year earlier Schmitty won five medals at the London Olympics. But at the Nationals she failed to place in any event, and that meant she also failed to qualify for that summer's World Championships, the biggest meet outside the Olympics. It was a mighty comedown for Schmitty, and we risked losing a once confident and dominant swimmer because of it.

That's when Michael stepped in and stepped up. He has known Schmitty for years. When he saw how disappointed and distraught she was, he pulled her aside and said, "Schmitty, this is what you do. Pull out a video of your races in London and watch them—and then use those races to visualize what you need to do to get back to where you were."

Perfect advice. At the 2015 Pan American Games, Allison won three gold medals and broke a thirty-six-year-old Pan Am mark in the 200-meter freestyle. A nice comeback, I would say.

RULE 3.6: GETTING USED TO RISK PREPARES YOU FOR LIFE'S BIGGER CHALLENGES.

In April 2015, one year after that meet in Mesa that I spoke about earlier, Michael returned to the same competition—but under much different circumstances. In the time that had passed, he enjoyed triumph but had also faced tumult. Yes, the comeback picked up momentum. He swam so well during the 2014 summer that he made the American team for the next World Championships, a key marker toward the bigger dream of competing in one more Olympics.

But in the early hours of September 30 Michael was pulled over by Baltimore police for speeding and crossing the double yellow line while driving in the Fort McHenry Tunnel. Sobriety tests showed that he was extremely intoxicated; he was arrested and charged with DUI. He later pleaded guilty and received a one-year suspended prison sentence and eighteen months of supervised probation. Subsequently, USA Swimming barred him from competition for six months and removed him from the World Championships team. The press and the Internet trollers, of course, had a field day eviscerating him during this period.

I didn't speak to him until the day after his arrest. When I finally reached him, I asked, "Michael, what happened?"

"I screwed up big-time," he said.

"You sure did," I said, unable to hide my anger.

His behavior was unconscionable, inexcusable. The pain he could have inflicted while driving in that state is unimaginable. Fortunately, no one was hurt—including Michael—but the damage had been done: His reputation was in tatters.

Remarkably, from this terrible situation I believe something good is already coming about. Michael spent forty-five days in a treatment center in Arizona. I visited him once while he was there, and I began to see a different person emerging, and that person continued to evolve even after he left the center. He was more talkative, a little more carefree, but in a good sense. He looked as though eighteen pieces of gold had been lifted from his back. You know, being hailed as the greatest Olympian of all time is a tremendous achievement; it can also be a huge, expectation-laced burden. Today, I see someone who isn't always looking over his shoulder. He's looking ahead. He has a chance to move on with his life in a positive way.

I bring this incident up in the context of risk-taking because I think Michael is on the road to more than recovery; he's showing others the power that comes with taking control of your life and your actions. After the arrest and the headlines, he could have chosen to abandon his comeback and step away from public scrutiny. Or he could have chosen a trickier route: Go back to the pool and risk being the subject of fans' stares and reporters' suspicious questions.

In Mesa, in April 2015, he opted to take the latter course.

Before he competed in that meet, he faced the reporters, who, as a year earlier, had plenty of questions for him. He took them all, and was more thoughtful and introspective and honest with his answers than I think I had ever heard him be before. At one point he admitted, "Have I screwed up? Yeah. A lot. I know I've hurt a lot of people. And it's been terrible." Later, when asked if he worried about the cynics and the skeptics, he said, "Everyone has the right to believe what they want. To me, I know how I am now and how I feel when I wake up every day. Of course, I'd like to show everybody in the world that I am in a different place. But I understand it's going to take a lot of time for me to be able to prove that I'm different. This week is the first week I can start that. And hopefully people can really see me for who I am and they can accept that. And if they can't, well, that's their choice."

He also announced, in no uncertain terms, that his dream was Rio 2016. "You guys heard it here first," he told the reporters, "like it's a big surprise." And, with that, he smiled, and the reporters chuckled.

I believe Michael is now swimming with a purpose beyond his medal count. Don't get me wrong; when he makes it to Rio, he'll want to win every race he enters. He's a competitive junkie, remember. But he also wants to show the world that he's not just a great swimmer; he's a person who understands that we all come with flaws, and we have to work to overcome them.

And every now and then we need to take a risk so we can do just that.

5

RULE 4: SHORT-TERM GOALS
LEAD TO LONG-TERM SUCCESS

Just before I broke up our post-Labor Day Road to Rio meeting and sent the swimmers off for that day's workout, I told them I had one more thing to give them beside words of wisdom and a pep talk. Throughout my address, I had been clutching a folder containing fifteen sheets of paper. Each sheet was a blueprint of sorts for building an Olympic athlete.

I walked around handing each swimmer his or her sheet, then warned them collectively: "Don't lose it. That's your road map to Rio."

No, this was not a printout of a map with driving, sea, and air routes from Baltimore to Brazil. This was a metaphorical map. But, in truth, I did suspect that this piece of paper could work just as well as any MapQuest itinerary for getting my folks to the Games. In the days and weeks prior to this meeting, I had worked with my staff—assistant coach Erik Posegay and athletic trainer Keenan Robinson—to put together this group-training plan. It didn't just set out our schedule for the next few days; it blocked out the next 1,068 days. Yes, the next *1,068 days*—all the way to the start of the Summer Games.

"Take a close look at this, everyone. *This* is the blueprint," I told the swimmers. "And understand one more thing: In the next week I'm going to sit down with you one-on-one and personalize this plan just for you."

When I did meet with each swimmer, we would project ahead to August 6, 2016, the first day of Olympic competition in Rio, and then work backward. We would slot in the major competitions that someone like Tom Luchsinger needed to swim before the Games. We would plot what projected goal times Lotte Friis should hit at different markers along the way. We would then get more nitty-gritty: We would have columns for the amount of training mileage each swimmer would need to swim per month over the next thirty-five months. We'd include what type of dryland workouts they should do and which targets they'd need to meet. We'd want Cierra Runge to be up to three sets of six pull-ups by Christmas of 2013; for the next twelve months we'd want Matt McLean lifting forty-pound weights at least twice a week during dryland. We'd dictate when they should start tapering—start easing back on their workouts—before certain competitions. We'd label the weeks we would be traveling to our high-altitude camp.

Basically, we'd set forth just about everything they

would need to do and every mark they would need to nail over the next three years. What might we leave out? Well, we'd let them determine when they would call home to their parents, when they would go to the bathroom, and when they would walk their dogs.

Otherwise, few things would be left to chance.

Matt later said that he had never seen such a detailed plan of attack—and this coming from a guy who had dreams of going into law enforcement once his swimming days were over. And Tom Luchsinger told someone, "No wonder Michael did so well."

All of this scheduling and prepping may have been novel to our new swimmers, but for Michael the game-planning was second nature. In fact, just as I was about to break up the meeting I glanced over at MP. He seemed nonplussed. He'd been here before, seen it before. He understood that a good part of his success had come from the planning and the goal-setting embedded in the sheet everyone was now holding. He took the paper, folded it into fours, put it in his backpack, and headed off downstairs to the pool.

It was 2:30 P.M. The day was already slipping away. He knew what was next. We had a schedule to keep.

RULE 4.1: GET YOUR G.P. (GAME PLAN) IN PLACE.

Henry David Thoreau has a quote that I often remind myself of at the start of a new day: "Do not worry if you have built your castles in the air. They are where they should be. Now put the foundations under them."

With those pieces of paper, I had given my swimmers a foundation to build their vision—that vision, of course, being a spot on the U.S. Olympic team.

As we've already discussed, a vision is the dream you want to accomplish, though I'm sometimes reluctant to use the word *dream,* because it conjures up fantasy or illusion. No, your vision should be attainable and achievable—provided that you have the All-In Attitude and a willingness to take some chances. And one more requirement: You need a means to get you there. Thoreau may have called it a foundation, but with the Method I call it the Game Plan, or G.P. As you'll see, your G.P. provides you with a strategy for transporting you to where you want to go, whether it's from the stockroom to the corner office, from a city-council job to one in the U.S. Capitol, or from a pool in Baltimore to one in Rio de Janeiro.

Your Game Plan must be well-thought-out, thorough, and a bit ambitious—just like the one I handed my swimmers. Okay, maybe not *that* ambitious. I can be a bit obsessive at times, and plotting the next 1,068 days certainly ranks high on the over-the-top scale. But here's the point: Your G.P. also can't be something you simply scratch out on the back of a supermarket receipt between reruns of *Law & Order.* Erik, Keenan, and I worked on our swimmers' schedules for several days, discussing the peculiarities of each athlete. We needed to consider outside commitments the swimmers had; some, for instance, must miss practice at points to make appearances for their sponsors.

Others, like Allison and Chase, had collegiate commitments on their dockets, so we had to tweak their plans some. As best we could, we considered every possibility, and factored them into the G.P.s.

And that's what you need to do: plan your Game Plan.

The extent of your G.P. will depend on the grandness of your vision. Earlier, I mentioned that you might have a vision of becoming an effective skier one day. Seems doable, seems practical—and it seems like something you could achieve by the last big winter snowstorm. But if that's the dream you can't start Game Planning in February. No, start in the summer, maybe with a little research. Ask some friends who are seasoned skiers for advice on getting started now. They might say that the summer is the ideal time to work on developing the upper-leg strength you'll need to handle the curves of a slope. You might also look into purchasing supplies at off-season discounts. And why not contact some ski instructors? It's summer; they have nothing else to do but talk. Tell them you want to take a ski vacation to Park City, Utah, next season. It's now July. What should you be doing to get ready?

But maybe you have visions with longer horizons. Perhaps you want to go back to school and get your MBA. Or you want to be promoted from a middle-management accounting position to a VP role. Or you finally want to write your memoir. Yes, those visions could take longer to achieve, but the Game Planning is the same. First, discover and determine what you'll need to do to eventually find success. Then take your findings and plot them into a G.P. model. Here's how I do it: Because I like to keep most things low-tech, I keep all data points I collect in the kinds of notebooks you might see a college kid using. Then, when it's time to make a G.P. for a swimmer, I pull out a day planner, look for dates of major competitions, and work in reverse, plugging in the key dates, workouts, anything I know my swimmer will need to accomplish en route to vision date.

To be honest, the G.P. isn't some newfangled elixir I'm offering up. For decades, university professors have given their students a syllabus at the start of every term, outlining what is expected of them each week until a final grade is given. Then there are toy-makers. They plot years in advance, conceiving games and dolls for Christmas seasons well into the future. Or consider recreational marathoners— the ones who take twice as long as the world's best to run 26.2 miles. They know that the finish line comes only after they've completed a sixteen-week training cycle.

These are all examples of G.P.s in action.

Simply put, the G.P. provides a rule book to follow and a schedule to keep, a pair of foundational piers that make achieving a vision possible, not illusory.

But, as simplistic a concept as the G.P. is, I'm constantly baffled by how few people conceive and use one. Case in point: Because I give a lot of talks to groups and offer my secrets for helping swimmers achieve their visions, I often meet non-swimmers who are excited to share their visions with me. When I hear these visions, I get excited, too. These people tell me how they want to be the No. 1 salesperson in their company or they want to make their varsity golf team or they want to read fifty books by year's end or they want to lose twenty-five pounds by the start of summer. When I hear the pitch, I tell them, "That's great! Go get it!" But then I immediately follow up with, "What's your plan of attack? What's your road map look like to get you to where you want to go? Do you have a Game Plan?" Too often, I get confused looks in return—and I realize something: These people have disappointment in their future, not fulfillment.

RULE 4.2: LET SHORT-TERM GOALS GUIDE YOUR G.P.

The best G.P.s, though, are not calendars on steroids. Sure, when developing a Game Plan you'll want to design it around certain time frames based on your life and what fills it up—work, your kids' events, nights out with friends, a vacation. But, beyond dates, you need one more vital thing: a set of short-terms goals that will serve as benchmarks on the road to your long-term success.

"Wait a minute," you're probably saying. "To achieve a dream goal you need other goals?" Well, in a word, yes.

Let me use another map analogy to show you what I mean. Say your vision is to become a Hollywood star, but you're living in a small town in the hills of North Carolina. You're 3,000 miles from the dream—daunting, to say the least. But you have the All-In Attitude and lots of desire.

So, in your '95 Honda Civic with 200,000-plus miles on the odometer, you take off one day because you've heard of a role in a summer-stock play being staged in Ottumwa, Iowa. It's a small part in a small town, but it's a start. You get the part and your reviews are good. When the run is over, someone tells you of another bit role in a show in even tinier Buffalo, Wyoming. You take off—and wow them again. Your stage presence is getting better, your timing is improving, you're less nervous with each performance. You're getting noticed more and more, too. A producer says he needs a headliner for a play he's putting on in San Jose. This time the role is bigger, the city is more cosmopolitan, and now you're actually in the state where you ultimately want to be.

You're taking small steps on the way to the big one.

I know of what I speak: I went to Florida State University with hopes of becoming either a classical pianist or an Olympic swimmer. Neither of these dreams materialized—not for lack of effort but for a shortage of talent. By the time I was a junior, though, I had realized that I had an interest in coaching. An assistant position opened up on the swim team's staff, and I grabbed it. I was in an excellent spot: working under Terry Maul, a highly respected college coach. In the back of my mind, I thought I could stay at Florida State and coach forever and be happy. But I could also get out on the road and learn from a lot of great coaches, developing my own personal coaching brand along the way.

Ultimately, I chose the second course, making my way across the country and then back, working at smaller clubs and then bigger ones, until I landed at the premier swimming program in America: the North Baltimore Aquatic Club. Each stop was a progressive step toward my dream destination of working with swimmers who wanted to be world champions.

But, whether your ultimate destination is Baltimore or Hollywood or Rio or some place just a few minutes from your current location, you can get there by devising a road map labeled with defined yet reachable markers. And, once you pass all those markers, your big marker—your vision quest—will be in sight.

RULE 4.3: SET PROGRESSIVE GOALS AS MICHAEL DOES (JUST AVOID THE CHICKEN WINGS).

Let me show you how I initially worked this goal-setting system into Michael's G.P.

In March of 1999, I decided that Michael, then thirteen, had better understand the process that he would need to follow to make his first Olympics, in Sydney, which was only nineteen months away. So one day when he was off from school I called Debbie at her office and said, "I'm going to get Michael and take him to lunch. You mind?" She had no objections, so I called Michael and told him I'd pick him up at noon. "Be ready. We're going to Bateman's," I said.

Bateman's is one of Baltimore's legendary bistros,

though *bistro* may be too fancy a word for a place that caters to the buffalo-chicken-wings crowd, of which Michael was already a card-carrying member. If Debbie had let him, Michael would be at Bateman's for breakfast, lunch, and dinner, and then return for a snack just before bedtime. So I knew this was the right spot to get him in the mood for what I was about to feed him.

When we got seated at the restaurant, I took out a sheet of paper and said, "Michael, the Junior Nationals are coming up this summer. What are your goals?"

Of course, he said, "I dunno." It wasn't too surprising. Remember, he was out with his coach, who wasn't necessarily his best buddy.

I said, "Well, let's come up with some. Let's pick three events. The fifteen-hundred-meter freestyle. The four-hundred-meter individual medley. The two-hundred-meter 'fly. Now, what are your goals for those?"

He said, "Well, I want to be under the national age-group records, I guess."

"Okay, what are they?"

By the time the first plate of wings had made it to our table, we had written on the paper the following times: 2:04.68 for the 200-meter 'fly, 4:31.72 for the 400-meter individual medley, and 16:00.00 for the 1,500-meter freestyle. And then I wrote the three things he had to do in practice to nail those times. They were very specific training plans, ones that would get him to his projected times provided he succeeded with the progressive steps. When I had finished writing this to-do list, and writing it very neatly, I said, "Here you go. Take this home and put it on your refrigerator."

He did as I said, and I suspect that he looked at the list a hundred times a day; back then he was eating non-stop. And from March to July he consistently completed all the workout plans we had devised. Each training goal we had established at Bateman's he nailed. And that set up the spectacular meet he had at the Junior Nationals in Orlando. In the three events, he swam 2:04.68 for the 200 'fly, 4:31.84 for the individual medley, and 16:00.82 for the 1,500—virtually the exact times we had discussed at Bateman's.

When we got back to Baltimore, I said to Michael, "Bring in that sheet from your refrigerator." There they were. And by writing down his vision (three record-setting times) along with preliminary goals (his training plan), he had learned to mentally match a goal with each workout. The goals were reasonable. They were challenging, probably at the top of his range, but not so unreasonable that he felt he couldn't reach them if he really pushed.

And from that point forward he started writing down all his goals—from the intermediary goals to his long-term vision—all the time.

RULE 4.4: MAKE GOAL-SETTING SOMETHING YOU CAN'T HIDE FROM.

Today, Michael is perhaps the most effective goal-setter I know. He's proved that to me, and to the world, plenty of times. Going into the 2008 Olympics, you may recall, his goal was to win eight gold medals. History shows that he nailed it. What has helped Michael is the fact that he can visualize a race, its time, and how he'll swim the event with incredible clarity based on what he has achieved prior to a championship. His ability to perform under the crushing pressure of Olympic competition is a direct result of the mental preparation and physical training he's done in the pool every day. You see, achieving intermediary, progressive goals on a regular basis produces everyday excellence—and keeps your Game Plan aligned with your vision.

Getting Michael to the point where he understood the value of regular goal-setting was a learning process, though. First, as I mentioned, I had to show him how to put pencil to paper and set intermediate goals. And then I had to remind him—as I still do with many of my swimmers—that you must keep setting goals as you move toward your ultimate one.

I'm a big believer in providing visual cues to keep my people focused both on their short-term goals and their long-term vision. We have a large whiteboard hanging in the meeting space at Meadowbrook. On it is listed every major swim meet scheduled during the Olympic cycle—along with the number of days until the event.

Let me tell you, the board knows how to deliver a kick in the tail. Too often I've seen a swimmer who has been a bit nonchalant with his workouts come into the office, look at the board, and say, "Holy . . . ! The Mesa Grand Prix is only *four weeks away!*" Come the next practice, he's moving with some extra kick.

Give yourself similar visual aids for the daily goals you want and need to achieve. For instance, say you're a sales rep and you're struggling to make your monthly quota of sales calls. You know the problem: You procrastinate at the start of the month, then need to blitz through a bunch of calls in the month's waning days. Sure, by month's end you can check off that you hit "Quantity," but how was the "Quality"? Iffy, I suspect. Here's the remedy: Get a big printout of a calendar month, and on the final day of the month write in big red numerals the number of calls you need to make by then. Let's say the number is one hundred. There are twenty or so workdays in the month, so you should average five calls a day. Work backward from the last day of the month, plugging in "5" in big red letters on each day. Tack that calendar sheet to your office wall so everyone who comes in can see it (especially you). Now, tell yourself, "I'm not going home at night until I put an *X* though the 5."

With the poster staring at you every morning, you'll make your mark—and you'll notice an improvement in the quality of your business.

RULE 4.5: LEARN FROM YOUR GOAL-SETTING BLUNDERS. (I SURE HAVE.)

As my swimmers will tell you, I'm very good at telling them what they need when taking the steps toward their goals.

Unfortunately, I'm not always good at following my own advice.

The story I'm about to share reveals, I think, the trouble you can get into when you don't establish meaningful goals as part of your G.P. It shows that, yes, you may get lucky and achieve your vision, but you may also pay along the way.

In my case, I had a dream of one day owning a business. The way I figured it, if I could be my own boss I could control my financial destiny. I also assumed that I would make a good businessman. I'd simply apply my skills as a swim coach—Game Planning, scheduling, ordering folks to do things ("Another twenty laps, people!")—to leading an organization. As I discovered (the hard way), running a swim practice is not the same as running a business.

Here's what happened: For four years, from 2004 to 2008, I coached the men's team at the University of Michigan. During that period, we produced some excellent squads and won a conference title. And while I was coaching the team I continued to coach Michael. Even though he wasn't a student, he trained at the university's aquatic center. In fact, Michael and I did most of our preparations for the Beijing Games on the Michigan campus.

But after the 2008 college season I was offered the chance to come back to Meadowbrook as the head coach of NBAC. Previously, I had been the No. 2 man under Murray Stephens, a legendary figure in the sport. The offer was tempting; Meadowbrook had had a history of producing great talent, going back to well before Michael began swimming there. Given MP's growing fame, we assumed that even more kids would want to train where the gold king swam. So the coaching position sounded fine. The hitch? I was at a point in my life where I was seeking new challenges and more income. I wasn't completely sure if "swim coach" still totally satisfied me. When I told Murray this, he said he had an idea: Now that he was retiring, he was looking to reduce his financial exposure. "Bob," he asked, "why don't you buy a stake in Meadowbrook?"

Hmm, I thought, this sounds intriguing.

So, along with Michael, we put up the money to lease the facility and to run our programs out of the club. My vision had come true. I was my own boss.

As they say, be careful what you wish for.

Meadowbrook has been around since 1930 and has served thousands of Baltimore families over the years. Sure, we're nationally known for hosting the North Baltimore Aquatic Club, the élite training program that Michael and Allison and the other Olympians have trained with. But we also have regular members—families, recreational swimmers—who use the club to cool off from the summer heat or to work out year-round in our indoor facilities. It's a pretty surreal sight: On a typical day, you'll see everyone from toddlers to AARP members swimming in the same pool as Olympians.

When I returned to Meadowbrook after the 2008 Olympics, many of the old-time members seemed glad to see me. In the first days back, I heard "Welcome back, Bob!"

and "Great job in Beijing!" plenty of times. (Michael had just completed his eight-gold-medal sweep.) But the members also started dropping a lot of not-so-subtle hints about what could be done around the place. They were asking for better showers in the locker rooms and renovations to the snack bar and new deck chairs for the outdoor pool. To everyone with a suggestion, I said, "Sure thing. Thanks for the idea. I'll look into it." And, as I investigated more closely, I realized that the place was in need of work. A lot of costly work.

I mumbled to myself, "Some dream come true." In fact, the word I should have used was *nightmare*.

Throughout my first year as boss, I lost plenty of sleep thinking about what needed to be done at Meadowbrook. Some nights I wondered where I had gone wrong. "Dang," I'd say to myself while tossing in bed, "this was the thing I always wanted to do—run my own shop. How could I be in such a mess?"

And then I realized: I hadn't prepared myself completely for the position I was now in and the responsibilities that came with it. I may have wanted this dream job, but I had failed to set the markers that would have prepared me for the reality. Had I studied any finance or accounting? *No.* Had I made a plan to research other swimming facilities and examine their operations? *No.* Had I studied the difference between coaching young kids and managing middle-aged employees? *No.* Had I set any goals for the club or for myself? *No, no, no.*

I had not developed a G.P. that would make my transition from swim coach to businessman a smooth one. The bottom line showed that. At the end of 2009—the end of my first year back at Meadowbrook—the numbers came in: The business had lost about $350,000 that year.

Toward the end of 2009, I decided to take a few days off. One night I told myself, "Okay, Bowman, you screwed up—but now set a plan of attack that will make this work in the long run." I knew that I needed to put the Method to work. During that break, and over lots of coffee, I designed a five-year business plan. For each year, I came up with target revenue and expenses figures. I indentified areas where the club functioned well, and where it needed help. I identified staffing needs, short-term and long-term. Ultimately, I came up with a vision: By 2014, I wanted Meadowbrook to be at breakeven or better.

I shared my G.P. and my vision with my lawyers and accountants and with Michael, my business partner. Everyone agreed that we had a road map.

The results? By 2014, I'm happy to say, Meadowbrook was no longer losing money. Okay, so we weren't making much, either, but at least we had stopped the bleeding. We were a leaner business in many ways, but you wouldn't notice that by looking at the club and all the improvements we had made. For the most part, the five-year plan had worked, and, soon enough, I was working on the next one.

From that experience, I "re-remembered" something: *Build toward a vision, don't rush to it.* The progressive steps—the intermediary goals—help train your mind to deal with challenges and expectations. Each goal you hit along the way will add to your confidence. In my case, I should have done more homework and learned more business skills if I fully intended to be a successful business operator. I needed a G.P. to guide me. Admitting this still annoys me.

Remember: You'll short-circuit your vision quest by taking shortcuts. Establish a G.P. and follow it.

RULE 4.6: EARN THE SUCCESS YOU ACHIEVE. YOUR G.P. WILL SHOW YOU HOW.

With my swimmers, I talk often about "deserving success." In fact, I don't just talk about it; I tweet about it. Consider the following messages from @coach_bowman:

"Just when you think you have seen it all . . . there are more challenges. #deservesuccess"

"Blame no one. Expect nothing. Do something. #deserve-success"

"For those of you with dreams of #Rio2016, the clock is ticking . . . #deservesuccess"

With those clues, can you figure out what I mean by "deserve success"?

If not, then just consider what I frequently tell a swimmer who stops by for a pep talk after a tough workout: "You have a dream you want to achieve, right? A world-record time. A place on the Olympic team. A medal. Great. Dream all you want. Envision everything you wish. But to get success you have to work for it. I have never met anyone who has achieved something by being static. You must be dynamic, and you must look at challenges as opportunities that will further engage you. By taking on challenges and meeting them, you're moving toward your ultimate destination. And when you get there it will mean that you deserve it. Got it?"

Normally, the swimmer will just nod. Then I'll say, "Good. Now, get out of here and get back to the pool and swim."

Ideally, that little talk helps revive him. More important, it reminds him that to push forward in life—whether in pursuit of a record-setting time or in search of a new career path—he needs to push beyond old marks and on to new ones. And when he does, and when he has achieved success, he will have earned it. He will deserve it.

See what I mean?

Let me use Chase Kalisz as an example of someone who deserves the success he's attained—and, if he keeps to the Game Plan, can expect more success in the future. I've known Chase for a decade, ever since he joined NBAC as a nine-year-old. He grew up an hour outside Baltimore, so that meant his parents did some heavy-duty driving to get him to practice each day (talk about deserving success). So far, the commuting has paid off. Chase may be the best young swimmer NBAC has produced since a fellow named Phelps.

At the start of our training for the Olympics, Chase told

me his vision: To win gold in the 400-meter individual medley in Rio. Talk about a lofty dream. He chose perhaps the toughest event; it requires that a swimmer do 100 meters of each stroke—butterfly, back, breast, and free—in succession. A killer quad. And no one has done it faster than Michael, who set the world record of 4:03.84 while winning gold at the 2008 Olympics.

I asked Chase, "For you to win gold, what will you need to do?"

He knew. "Break Michael's record, Bob."

"Yep," I said, "and that's going to be a huge challenge. But if you do, you know what? You'll deserve success."

Chase nodded, then asked, "Okay, but how do I do it?"

And I told him. "You're not going to just break Michael's record; you're going to fly by it. You are going to swim a 4:00 IM."

When Chase heard that, he nearly turned purple. His personal best, at that point, was 4:09.22.

I set the bar so high because I wanted Chase to understand the challenge ahead of him. It was going to take tremendous effort to achieve what he wanted. Sure, I could have put him on a training plan that got him to the 4:02 mark, enough to break Michael's record. But out in the world beyond Meadowbrook a swimmer may be thinking, *I need to go 4:01*. And if that's the case not only does Chase not get gold; he doesn't get a record.

That's why I gave him an outrageous goal to focus on.

We established progressive goal times to measure improvement during the three-year training cycle. By the end of the 2014 collegiate season, his second at the University of Georgia, Chase had set an American record in the 400-yard individual medley. Yes, that was in yards, not the Olympic meters standard. But it was still a record. That summer, though, he backtracked. His improvement stalled; he seemed to be too relaxed in workouts.

Fortunately, he still had two years to get the intensity back—and he worked hard to do just that. The next summer, at the 2015 World Championships, his last major international meet before the Olympic Trials, Chase won a bronze medal in the individual medley. No, his time was far from Michael's record, but he proved that he could compete on the world stage. And so determined was Chase to be ready for the Trials (and, ideally, Rio), he decided to take a year off from Georgia and move to Tempe with me to train. Together, we're going to keep working to trim those seconds off his time. And when he hits his goal, he will #deservesuccess.

As Chase's story reveals, another benefit of developing a Game Plan is that you gain a scorecard that tells you definitively whether or not you're moving toward your vision. Too often, I hear from friends, "I tried this diet, but it didn't work. I'm still exactly the same weight as when I started." Well, they didn't deserve to lose the weight because they cheated all the time. Or I'll hear one of my younger swimmers complain about a high school teacher. "He's terrible. He gave me another C. I deserved at least a B." No, I think to myself, you didn't work hard enough to get a B.

Listen, you can't just hope that a gold medal, a good grade, or a promotion is waiting for you at the end of a cycle. You must do everything in your power—in your Game Plan—to make sure you deserve that reward.

RULE 4.7: BE PREPARED TO REVIEW YOUR GAME PLAN AND RESET YOUR GOALS.

I'm fortunate. Most days I go to work in a T-shirt, a pair of shorts, and running shoes. In my world, every day is casual Friday. And, not having worked in a corporate setting, I've generally avoided formal performance reviews as well. When my friends who do have office jobs tell me that their annual review is coming up, they may as well be saying that Mr. Grim Reaper is at the front door making an unexpected house call.

I wonder, Why all the stress? Sure, I can see the angst that might come with getting a grade on a past performance, a performance that stretches back six to twelve months. But maybe therein lies one problem with performance reviews. If a manager waits that long to tell an employee what she did right or wrong, then *he* should be worried about his job. Around Meadowbrook, my swimmers understand the deal: If you're doing good work, I won't say a thing, except maybe the occasional "Good job" or "Attagirl" or "Attaboy." I try not to overwhelm my swimmers with praise—and they know that. But if they mess up I tell them right away. I'm a big believer in instant and constructive feedback. And if I see the need to give a swimmer even more follow-up, I'll meet with her after practice and share what I think. I don't wait for a midyear review.

The other problem with a performance review? The name. I don't like *review*. If I'm going to the trouble of planning time to meet with a swimmer or an employee, I'd rather do a performance *preview*, not a review. That twist says, "We're looking ahead, not back. Sure, let's not forget what has occurred, but let's learn from it, and let's use it to adjust our Game Plan to build for the future."

The performance preview is essentially a chance to rethink the Game Plan; you don't want to try and move forward with an antiquated plan. Maybe you've already exceeded some of the progressive goals in your original plan, or maybe you failed to meet them. The preview allows you to rethink the steps you want to take in order to reach your vision.

History shows that adjusting a Game Plan can, in fact, lead to making history.

Let's go back to that meeting I had with Michael and his parents when he was only eleven. You'll recall that I set out the possibility that there could be something quite special in Michael's future when it came to competitive swimming. I told them he was bound to be an Olympian, most likely by 2004. What happened? Michael blew up those plans by making the 2000 Olympics as a fifteen-year-old, the youngest male American Olympian since 1932.

Suddenly, he was a star in the making.

In fact, in the run-up to the 2004 Athens Games he went from swimming phenom to worldwide sensation, in part because of an ingenious marketing gimmick devised by Speedo and Peter Carlisle, his agent at Octagon, the global marketing firm that represents dozens of Olympic athletes. Speedo, which already had Michael under a sponsorship deal, offered him a $1 million bonus if he matched Mark Spitz's record of seven golds in a single Olympiad.

"The million-dollar offer has captured the public's fancy," Stu Isaac, Speedo's senior vice president of marketing at the time, told *USA Today*. "It's also helped elevate Michael to a level where people are saying, 'This guy must be for real.'"

Indeed, the ploy put Michael in the public eye, but in the end he won *only* six gold medals. The bonus was put on hold.

But after Athens I got to thinking, We went into these Olympics with a chance for seven golds. What do we have to do to make that possibility more realistic?

I then conducted a performance preview, which led to an adjustment in our Game Plan for Beijing. In the years leading up to those Games, I had Michael on a workout regimen that put him on pace to win not seven, not eight, but nine gold medals. Eventually, we realized that the actual Olympic swimming schedule made it virtually impossible for MP to go for nine, but our revamped Game Plan had still done the job. Michael not only matched Spitz's record of seven golds but bettered it by one.

Michael made history, and collected his $1 million bonus, because he wasn't beholden to a past Game Plan—and neither should you be.

Look, things are going to come up in your world that will force you to tinker with your career or your life strategy. A co-worker, for instance, may leave unexpectedly, creating an opportunity for you to move up the organization chart sooner than you'd expected. Or a spouse may get a new opportunity in another part of the country, forcing you to leave your job and curtail your rise up the company ladder. I know, stuff happens.

My advice: Expect stuff to happen. That way, you'll be ready to react to it—with a new Game Plan, a new set of short-term goals, and a renewed effort to get you to where you ultimately want to go.

6

RULE 5: LIVE THE VISION EVERY DAY

I hate making predictions, and yet I'm consumed by predictability.

How's that for a brainteaser? Let me take a second to explain what I mean.

Sportswriters will often ask me to give a prediction on how one of my swimmers will do in a race. I always say, "I'm not going there." That's because when you make such a prediction you're setting up an expectation that's out of your control. Who's to know, for instance, if an opponent has trained better than your athlete has. Such forecasting is fraught with disaster.

I know of what I speak.

I can think of three or four times in my coaching career when I've made predictions, and each time I was left humbled. The most recent occurrence came in 2012. One day before Michael and I headed to the London Games, we sat in my office at Meadowbrook and discussed whether he should compete in the 400-meter individual medley. He had won Olympic gold twice before in the event, even setting a world record in Beijing. Granted, his training for London hadn't been as smooth as it had been in past Olympic cycles, but in my heart—if not my mind—I thought he was plenty ready to race competitively. So on that day we agreed that he'd swim the individual medley, with the last words out of my mouth being, "What's the worst thing that could happen? You win a silver medal? You'd never do worse than that."

Well, we soon found out that he sure could. Michael finished fourth in the event; he won no medal, the first time since the 2000 Olympics that he had failed to make the podium in an event.

Yes, he was physically ready to compete in the race; I had made sure of that even with the craziness that had preceded the Games. But there were things I could not be sure of: how his competition had trained, how he might react to the London setting, where his confidence stood. Fortunately, missing the podium snapped Michael into focus. From that point forward, he went on to win four golds. Even so, I won't be making any predictions anytime soon.

But when it comes to predictability—well, that's a whole other matter.

The goal for my program, as it is for most organizations, is to work toward results that are predictable and manageable. The companies that regularly top the Fortune

500—Walmart, Apple, GE—take predictable paths toward revenue targets, and that keeps them perpetually strong. It's the same thing with some college basketball teams. Duke and Michigan State, for instance, are seemingly always ranked high in pre- and post-season polls because their coaches have brought predictability to the way they manage their programs. Yes, as I've mentioned, you can never be one hundred percent sure of a final outcome, but your likelihood for success is heightened when you work through a method that has a track record of achievement.

In my case, I want my athletes to know that if they can go through the Method I've laid out for them, then the odds of reaching their visions will increase significantly. I establish this process based on the vision and the goals we've put forth, but it requires the athletes to commit all their effort (or as much as possible) on a consistent and almost daily basis. It can't be dolloped out at one's discretion.

Yes, it requires everyday excellence.

But the added lynchpin to this Method is that you can exert a good bit of control over the process—and control leads to even greater predictability. You dictate how hard you work on a project, when you will study for an exam, how dedicated you'll be to a diet. You don't worry about how much others are training or how much studying a fellow classmate is doing; you worry about you, your effort, and what you need to do in order to achieve your vision.

Now that we've established the need to have a dream

vision and supporting goals, and we've discussed the value of an All-In Attitude and a tolerance for taking (some) risk, it's time to establish the rules that will help you incorporate these qualities into your daily life. Here's the deal: If you want to have success, you need to wake up each day (or, at least, most days) with that mission near the top of your agenda. You won't be alone. I've found that most high performers plot daily priorities and tasks, attack them in a predictable, controlled manner, and then reflect on their effort at day's end to see if the latest results align with their long-term vision.

Yes, such a process can be rigorous, and it can be depleting. I know. I've coached many Olympians. I've also had my share of swimmers who could not keep up. They had the talent to be here, just not the everyday commitment. As such, they eventually moved on.

Those who stayed? Predictably, they've moved forward and toward excellence.

RULE 5.1: SUCCESS BECOMES ROUTINE WHEN YOU HAVE A ROUTINE.

So far, I've talked quite a bit about the swimmers I coach. For a moment, let me tell you about my own swimming career.

I didn't become a competitive swimmer until I was eleven, which, in many respects, is late if you want to have a shot at being recognized on the national level (remember, Michael began swimming at five). That said, I took to swimming the way . . . well, okay, the way a fish takes to water. I couldn't get enough of the sport, or of what was required to get better at it. And, admittedly, to become a great swimmer you need to put in hours of training, hours that are unlike those for any other sport. This fact I learned one summer in my hometown of Columbia, South Carolina.

Scott Woodburn, my coach in high school and during the summer, had a particular drill that he made his swimmers do. It came at the same time and the same place every week during the summer. We would go to Williams-Brice Stadium at the University of South Carolina (the same one that draws eighty thousand football fans to Gamecocks games in the fall), and at exactly three o'clock in the afternoon, and with the summer sun in full force, and with no one there but the grounds crew tending to the football field, he made us run all the stadium's steps. After that bit of agony, we would go to the gym and do weight work. Then we'd go to the pool and swim for two and a half hours. Finally, at 9 P.M. he'd let us collapse.

It was pure torture—and total exhilaration.

Scott's workout was enough to get us fit and keep us fit, and drill into my head the kind of routine I would need to go from good to very good. Unlike some other hobbies that seemed to come to me naturally, such as playing the piano and the trombone, swimming required extra effort on my part. So I put in the hours of practice. I studied the techniques of every stroke. I spent added time with my coaches asking questions, and then more questions.

Eventually, the effort paid off. I earned a small scholarship to Florida State, but I also learned a lifelong lesson: En route to your dream vision, you need to put in the effort on an almost daily basis.

One of my favorite quotes comes from the champ Muhammad Ali. At one point during his career, he said, "The fight is won or lost far away from witnesses—behind the lines, in the gym and out there on the road, long before I dance under those lights." Ali obviously knew what he was talking about; he won the heavyweight title three times.

What Ali is saying is much like what I tell my athletes— and what I tell professionals of all types when I talk to them about their visions. Whether you are a doctor, a student, or a parent, your daily "workout" plan is just that: a prescription for work. A coach, a professor, a boss may give you guidance or suggest a plan, but you're the one who controls it; you decide how much effort to put into something.

I hold that successful people have figured out a routine that produces the right level of effort. If you work in a sales organization, for instance, check out last year's Gold Circle members. I predict—okay, I suspect—that their everyday output is measurably better than that of other sales reps. On a daily basis, they prospect more, close more deals, follow up with customers more frequently than other team members do. And they execute these tasks with as much focus on a Friday as they exhibit on a Monday. Similarly, consider the pre-med student who's pulling A's by studying organic chemistry two hours a day, not just two hours before the final exam. Or the writer who's composing two thousand words a day, not two hundred. Or the budding heavyweight champion who's doing extra speed-bag work when he could be grabbing a nap or having lunch.

Or the high school swimmer who's attacking the stairs of Williams-Brice Stadium, and not giving in to the steamy South Carolina summer.

As I said, running those steps was difficult, as were the early-morning swim practices my mom would drive me to. When I was a teenager, I would swim 7,000 meters a day, and often see just a minuscule improvement in my times. Too often I would finish practice, trudge back to Mom's car, and start whining about how hard the sport was. Mom kept her cool, waiting until I finally shut up to say, "Bobby, when the season is over you can quit the team. But for now you've made a commitment and you're going to complete it in the best way possible."

Mom knew best. I wasn't aware of it at the time, but with each run up those stairs, and with each trip back to the pool for another 7,000 meters of work, I was setting myself up for success.

RULE 5.2: MAKE A SCHEDULE—AND STICK TO IT.

Two things you should know about me: I'm a morning person and I am a man of my routine.

I almost always wake up by 4:30 A.M., and then I lie in

bed until the alarm goes off at 4:45. (I set one just in case.) I read once that Descartes came up with some of his best theories by lying in bed in the morning. You're relaxed, and your brain is warming up; your creative juices are starting to flow, as they say. With my fifteen minutes I think about the day ahead—what I want to do, what I'd like to accomplish, and how to get myself organized. It's truly the perfect downtime.

With my mind now cranking, I'm ready to get the body moving. I head downstairs for breakfast, the same meal almost every day. I get a measuring cup and pour in one serving of Ezekiel cereal. (Before I started measuring the amount, I must have been downing three or four servings, way too much for a middle-aged guy trying to keep his waistline in check.) I mix the cereal with organic yogurt, a couple of Craisins, five pecan halves—not four, not six, but five—and a little almond milk to loosen it up. Like I said, I have my routines.

By 5:15 A.M., I'm on the road to the pool, arriving by 5:45 A.M. I head to my office and start to design the morning practice session, which starts at exactly 7 A.M. I write the plan in longhand on a piece of graph paper; I never type it on my laptop. I've found that the act of putting pen to paper gives me a better feel for what I'm expecting from the swimmers. That's how I've been writing plans for twenty years: ballpoint pen on graph paper. I have graph-paper pads with practice plans going back to my earliest jobs. I'll refer to them often, but each day I write a new workout plan. I want to make sure "Today's Plan" fits into my plan for the week, my plan for the month, my plan for the next few years.

By 6:25 A.M. or so, devising the workout is almost complete. It lays out exactly which sets the swimmers will be doing and at what pace. It notes when we will be moving from one distance to another—say, from 25-meter sprints to 50-meter kick sets. It will detail the splits they need to hit during 200-meter butterfly legs. Nearly every second of the ninety-minute workout is accounted for.

I'll review the plan, though I rarely change a thing. Still, I'm not done. I always scribble a motivational quote at the bottom of the sheet to give the swimmers an extra kick.

This is the workout plan. This is the day's formula for adding fuel to my swimmers' Rio aspirations.

By 6:30 A.M., I've handed the sheet off to one of my assistants so that he can make copies for everyone. I have thirty minutes to check emails, get some paperwork in order, finish a second cup of coffee. Let's call it Bob Time.

At 7 A.M., and now down on the pool deck, I press a button and the large pace clock starts clicking. The swimmers dive in. Execution of the plan begins. And when the morning workout is over . . . ? Yes, I head to my office to plot the afternoon practice.

As you can see, it's a pretty regimented process. It's a procedure that might vary only if I'm traveling or taking a day off. But it works for me—and for my swimmers. Such preparation sends a signal to them that if they want success they need to work a plan.

Allison Schmitt has six Olympic medals, and she has earned every one. But she would be the first to tell you that she needs a routine like the one I put her on to get—and keep—her in prime shape. We know what happens when she doesn't follow such a regimen. I told you about her poor performance at the 2013 USA National Championships. Well, that came after a period when Schmitty was still away at school and training mostly on her own. Her routine slipped, and so did her effort.

When new swimmers join our program, my regimen and my attention to detail catches some off-guard. Even those coming from élite programs have never experienced such exactness. Here's an example of our precision: On most Tuesday afternoons, Keenan, my strength coach, has the swimmers do a thirty-minute leg workout. There's a reason for doing the drill then. He knows that three days later, on Friday, I will have them in the pool doing a kick set. For thirty to forty minutes, all they're doing is hanging on to kickboards and motoring up the length of the pool and back. Keenan and I have determined that the fifty or so hours between his drill and my drill is the optimal spread in order to produce maximum results.

I never put in a set just to be a tough guy. Every drill has a desired effect—to build stamina, add speed, maybe just build confidence. Most of all, though, the daily plan is part of my overall plan to keep my athletes working toward their primary goal.

As you're looking to fulfill the goals that will lead to your dream vision, consider how you can develop a daily schedule that will allow you to fit in the work you need to do. I don't expect everyone to wake up at 4:30 A.M. to map out the day. But you do need to plan. Say you want to lower your golf handicap from eighteen to single digits by Labor Day. Then you'd better set aside thirty minutes each day to practice your putting. Or say you want to read all of Dickens's classics by year's end. Then you'd better allot (at least) forty minutes of reading time each day. Or say you want to be in position to take over for your company's human-resources director when she retires in six months. Then you'd better use some time each day to get up to speed on the legal policies by which your company must abide.

The act of scheduling activities that are key to your vision will give structure to your overall plan. If you don't believe me, just listen to my swimmers.

RULE 5.3: BRING PURPOSE TO YOUR PURSUIT EVERY DAY.

After a practice one day, Jessica Long was talking to someone about life as an NBAC swimmer. She and her teammates had just finished a very difficult workout. We had a competition coming up in about three weeks, so I wanted to push them a little harder in preparation. One set included a heavy load of 25-yard butterfly sprints. I had them do twenty laps, each one on a twenty-second interval; this gave them about five seconds of rest between each lap. No, not easy. Besides a dolphin kick, butterfly requires a repetitive arms-over-head maneuver to get propulsion. Imagine running 25 yards with bags of groceries raised above your head. Imagine doing that twenty times very fast. That will give you a sense of the intensity of this drill.

Jessica had to work even harder to keep up because, without legs, most of her butterfly movement comes from her shoulders and arms. She had reason to whine. Instead, she later told someone, "I know that Bob is the best coach in the world. I truly believe that or else I wouldn't be putting up with these really hard workouts and coming here day in and day out." She paused for a moment, then added, "One thing has really stuck with me: I really love how he talks about being an élite athlete 24/7, three hundred and sixty-five days of the year. I never thought of it like that before."

In any pursuit, you need to bring a sense of purpose to it. I'm not suggesting that there shouldn't be any fun or laughs in what you do—especially if you're in a world like mine. I try never to forget that I'm coaching a sport, and that sports should be enjoyable. But I also know that my swimmers have pledged, at least to themselves, that for this window in their lives swimming is their livelihood. Because of that, I want them to think of themselves as professionals, with the responsibilities of a professional. That means don't miss work, be on time, do your job according to the standards expected.

That said, I also know that outside distractions may get in the way of their profession. Here's what I mean: Few in swimming make the millions through endorsements that Michael has (winning twenty-two Olympic medals will do that). Most of my professional swimmers need to make money while they're training. Their monthly income may often be just the couple of thousands of dollars they get from the likes of a swimsuit sponsor. With such deals, though, come potential conflicts. For instance, one morning Matt McLean came to me after practice and told me that he would have to miss the next group workout. I gave him the scowl. Matt's one of those swimmers who could be podium-bound in Rio, but not if he misses a lot of work.

"No, Bob, it's not like that," he quickly said when he saw me flinch. "I have to be in Boston Monday afternoon for a sponsor. But here's my plan: I'll be at the pool early Monday morning and do a workout on my own."

With those words, Matt avoided the doghouse—and also demonstrated his professionalism. He proved to me that even though his schedule had changed, his priorities hadn't.

That is the kind of foresight you'll need as you work the plan toward your vision. Life, as we know, can play dirty tricks on us. But don't let those tricks become excuses. When devising a daily plan, be both strategic and flexible. In fact, when you first start scheduling your days and including time to work on goals, keep track of how those initial days go. How often was one day disrupted by unexpected distractions? When were your mind and your body best suited to executing a daily goal? Where was the ideal location for you to work on your goal? Take note of what you discover, and then use that information to shape your daily plans going forward.

In an unpredictable world, bring some predictability to it.

RULE 5.4: PREDICTABLE PERFORMANCE DEPENDS ON CONSISTENT EFFORT.

As I described earlier, I have my quirky routines, but I'm not the only coach who does. Consider Jim Harbaugh, the head football coach at the University of Michigan. When he was playing football, Harbaugh never wanted to be late for practice. In fact, Nick Baumgardner, a reporter for *The Ann Arbor News*, tells the story that Harbaugh ensured his promptness by timing himself while tying his shoelaces in the locker room; that drill indicated to Harbaugh how much time he needed to allot for those dastardly laces—information he could then use when planning his daily schedule. He's also known for wearing khaki pants on the sidelines day in and day out. He explained the reason to ESPN: "It's gotten to the point where I save so much time a day knowing that I don't have to stand in front of the closet trying to decide what outfit to pick out. [I save] about fifteen to twenty minutes a day—that adds up day after day."

That's my kind of guy.

Idiosyncrasies aside, Harbaugh has a record that shouts success, and that's why Michigan paid him a lucrative salary to leave professional football in order to turn the once storied Wolverines back into national championship contenders. Harbaugh's résumé says he can do just that. Previously, he needed just two seasons to remake the doormat San Francisco 49ers into Super Bowl runners-up. That followed his elevation of the Stanford University football team from a middling squad to a major college power.

What's Harbaugh's turnaround secret?

Well, of course he knows his sport; he's the son of a football coach, he played college and pro ball himself, and his brother, John, is the head coach of my favorite team, the Baltimore Ravens. But people who know Jim say the trait he demands of himself—a consistent day-in, day-out effort—is what he expects of his players, and he wants them to bring to the practice field the same energy and focus that they bring on game day. He means it. Following his first workout with his new team, he told his players, "Every day there will be an evaluation process, on every player, in every drill."

Like Jim Harbaugh, I constantly stress to my athletes that they can't do B practices and then expect to turn in an A performance on race day. You need to bring a mindset to your everyday job or passion—whether it's swimming or accounting, gardening or consulting—that is focused on doing exceptional work. Michael exuded that trait. When he was coming up in the sport, that was how he distinguished himself from his teammates on a daily basis. At most workouts he would earn 8s (an A on my scorecard). Even though he might show up to a 7 A.M. practice with a scowl on his face (MP is not a morning person), once he was in the water Michael would be the picture of concentration and determination. There are even videos of him as an eleven-year-old motoring up a lane and leaving teammates in his wake during a practice set that was intended to be easy. Of course, every now and then MP would falter and deliver a dud of a practice. The thing was, he would rarely repeat such a showing on consecutive days. By the next morning, he would be back to receiving a grade of 8.

His consistent everyday effort was as remarkable as his natural talent.

It's pretty simple: The more consistency you bring to your daily goal work, the more predictable your success will be, whether you're chasing football titles, Olympic medals, or wins in your day-to-day life.

RULE 5.5: PATIENCE IS A VIRTUE WHEN PURSUING A GOAL.

I mentioned my father, Lonnie Bowman, earlier, and I said that he was a man who didn't take too many big risks in life. Well, I'd like to amend that assessment a bit.

Back when I was maybe three or four years old, Dad decided to go back to college. Suddenly, he was attending classes all morning and afternoon and then heading to a local Sears store to work the night shift in the hardware department. A risky move, indeed. He could have stayed in the job he had and we would have made ends meet. But he saw the college degree as a means to a better way of life for my mom, my sister, and me. Then, once he'd earned his college degree, Dad went back and got a master's. He eventually used his degrees to get a high-level job in the state government that he would hold for thirty years.

During that stretch when Dad was going to school and working nights, I didn't see much of him, but I still learned a great lesson from him: pursuing a dream requires a steady, one-day-at-a-time approach. He knew the potential value of those degrees, and he also knew that they could not be achieved overnight. Instead, he and Mom worked out a system that allowed him—given the limited time that a father with two kids may have—to squeeze as much as he could out of every day. When you make a commitment to something, you give one hundred percent.

Part of the trick to achieving a goal is knowing that it will require stick-to-itiveness. For instance, take getting a promotion at work. Yes, to earn one you need to prove yourself on the job, but it may also require putting in the time and waiting for an opening to come up. Or how about buying a dream house in a prime neighborhood? That may take years of putting a lot of small deposits in the savings account before there's enough for the down payment. Or how about learning to play Beethoven's Violin Concerto on the piano? To master that, you'll first need to learn those dreaded scales and then the arpeggios.

Work, time, and luck come with achieving a goal. Just know that if you pursue your goal with a steady drumbeat, the length between start and success will continually shrink.

RULE 5.6: THAT SAID, YOU CAN ALSO RAMP UP YOUR PURSUIT.

As much as I may promote the steady-as-you-go approach, I can also see the value in accelerating the process. Consider what Michael did en route to his record-setting achievements.

To repeat, Michael loved to practice. In the first ten years that I coached him, I suspect that he missed only five practices. He was that consistent. In fact, he did more than not miss a practice; he created more opportunities to practice.

Here's one example: With most swim programs, you work out Monday through Saturday and take Sunday off. But back when Michael was just starting out it wasn't always easy to find practice time on weekdays, so he began swimming on Sundays. Well, the habit never stopped— even when pool time became more available. As a result, he was practicing seven days a week, and that meant that he was training as much as fifty more days a year than his competition. Now, just do the math: Over a four-year cycle leading up to an Olympics, Michael swam two hundred days more than his primary competition. One day he said to me, "Bob, we're getting five years of training into everyone else's four years. Not too shabby."

Now, for sure we didn't swim every day. For instance, we took Christmas off. Well, let me rephrase that: We *used* to take Christmas off. Sorry, but indulge me with one more story. When Michael was fifteen and increasingly making a name for himself in the sport, I actually scheduled practice on Christmas Day. He had a meet scheduled for early January in Europe, and I felt that he needed the work. We did a fairly easy practice, maybe an hour, and then we went back to the Phelpses' house and Debbie made Christmas Day brunch. In the scheme of things, the workout was nothing too outlandish.

Fast-forward to the next summer, when Michael swam exceptionally well at a major meet, and some of the older swimmers took notice. Afterward, we were all on the bus heading back to the hotel when a few swimmers approached us. "Man, we hear you train on Sunday—is that true?" one of them asked. Michael sheepishly nodded yes. Then another swimmer asked, "Do you ever take a day off? You must take Christmas off, right?"

Michael looked at me. I looked at him. "Nope, we practice on Christmas, too," Michael told the guys. Their faces turned yellow.

When we got off the bus, Michael whispered to me,

"I guess we're going to keep swimming on Christmas because these guys think it's nuts?"

"Yeah, we definitely are," I fired back, and we both started laughing. (We ended up swimming on Christmas for about six years until we came to our senses.)

Don't get me wrong: I tell these stories not too suggest that the pursuit of your goals should be an all-consuming, twenty-four-hour-a-day obsession. No, that is a recipe for burnout. My point is this: Success in any endeavor is often dictated by how much quality time and effort you put into it. Take the steady approach, like my dad, and you'll get there; try the souped-up approach, like Michael, and you'll also get there. Whichever route you take, just be mindful of the importance of quality and quantity. When it comes to daily effort, the more of both you put in, the better the results will be.

I tell my swimmers that each time they put in a little extra effort during practice they're making a deposit in their vision account. That account works like a savings account: The more you put in, the more your talent or skill will grow.

RULE 5.7: APPLY A LITTLE PRESSURE. IT WILL GO A LONG WAY.

As a coach of people who will one day be performing in front of fans and TV audiences and against high-level competition—essentially, in pressurized situations—I feel that I need to apply a certain degree of pressure during their daily training so that my swimmers are ready for the stress of race day. In a sense, I want race day to seem normal, or as normal as a major competition can be, and I want my swimmers to feel comfortable, not on edge.

How do I apply the pressure? Here's one way: When necessary, I let them know during practice how they're doing in a nice, LOUD voice.

I often hear friends in the "real world" talk about the boss who yells too much at meetings or behind closed doors. That he is "an ogre." Well, I would never endorse anyone who yells for the sake of yelling or creates a hostile workplace with his volume or tone; as a mentor or boss or coach, you are looking to instruct, not intimidate, your people. But I do think that there comes a time when a change of tenor can say something beyond the actual words spoken. The change says this: *We need to mix things up, because what we have now isn't working.*

I have a few set phrases that, combined with a bellow, alert people that they need to step up their effort. Here's one: When I want to single out one swimmer, I will go right up to him and simply say, "This is not acceptable! Come back tomorrow when you're ready to give me the effort I deserve!" There's no ambiguity in that delivery. Sometimes, though, I want to send a subtler but still pointed message. For instance, if I see a number of swimmers collectively not pushing it in practice, I'll yell, "We're having a serious lack of imagination today! Let's turn it up a little bit! You have high goals, but you need to do better if you plan to reach them. And you *can* do better!"

High performers know they need to keep improving, know they need to be pushed. But I've learned that not everyone responds to the same kind of pressure. As a coach who is trying to get my swimmers to reach their individual level of excellence, I need to know which athlete reacts best to which type of pressure I apply. With Michael, I tend to go with a more in-the-face approach. Yes, he'll push back, but he'll usually respond with an "I'll show you" effort. Allison Schmitt, on the other hand, has a more docile personality. If I went with the Michael approach, she would recoil. I've learned to find a more suitable way to push her.

Regardless of the approach I use, my goal is the same: My athletes come to me because they believe I can help them reach their goals. The pressure I apply is part of the path to making them ready. It's not unlike the intensity some professionals face in their job training. On their way to becoming firefighters, for instance, trainees undergo tests that simulate what might occur during an actual fire. Such procedures have a purpose: to make the fire personnel ready for the real thing.

Overall, I believe successful people are much better when pressure is placed on them during the process. The end result: When they later face a situation where they need to react and excel—during an important job interview, for example, or at a piano recital or in an Olympic swim race—they will understand the situation and how best to respond to it.

RULE 5.8: LOOK BACK OVER TODAY. IT WILL MAKE TOMORROW THAT MORE PRODUCTIVE.

My days, obviously, are long ones. Waking up at 4:30 A.M. makes that automatic. I do try to head home by 4:30 P.M., but even though I'm no longer at work, my day is not done. Usually, I'll pour a glass of wine, sit down, and think back over the past twelve hours. I assess what went well and what went poorly, what we achieved, and where we need to improve.

In a way, it's like watching the old TV evening news.

These days, everyone is constantly bombarded by information—via Twitter and Facebook, via conversations in scheduled meetings and in ad-hoc ones, via email and texts. We have so much "news" running through our heads, and yet we don't compartmentalize or edit it.

I think we need to. That way, we can make sense of everything—and make use of it, too. Just as Walter Cronkite would synthesize the day's events for America in twenty-two minutes each night, I look at my personal end-of-day debriefing as a perfect way to consider "what just happened" and prepare myself for tomorrow's installment. If I don't, all of what I did on a given day becomes useless clutter.

Part of my routine, as I mentioned earlier, is filing away

my practice plan from that day. I learned this trick from one of my earliest coaches. One day, when I was working with Paul Bergen, who coached such Olympic stars as Tracy Caulkins, he called me into his office and said, "Here, I'm going to give these to you, but you can never share them with anyone. They're only for you." They were copies of his training plans from 1978, the year he coached Caulkins to six gold medals at the World Championships. At the same meet, two of his other high school swimmers won gold as well. Many swimming experts consider Bergen's record at the meet the finest ever by a coach. Bergen so valued his practice plans that I had to swear to him, "No one will ever see these but me." If you were a Civil War historian, it was like being handed Ulysses S. Grant's secret diaries.

Of course, unless you're a swim nut, Bergen's papers held very little meaning. But I'm a nut, and they prompted me to start tracking the events of my daily work—and you should, too.

The notes I scribble have become my daily report card, a ranking of how the day went, what I did right and what I don't want to repeat again. You see, with "everyday excellence" you're attempting to be excellent *every day*. Obviously, that's not possible. But you also want to avoid repeating mistakes. My recordkeeping has helped me to do just that.

It works in all kinds of pursuits. I've read that such historical luminaries as Ben Franklin and Andrew Carnegie kept journals that they updated each day. Of lesser fame is Lori Shontz. She swam competitively throughout much of her early life, and now in middle age she continues to find time to squeeze in 2,000 or so meters a few days a week. But what mostly fuels her time these days is her passion for teaching journalism. She came to teaching after years as a sports reporter, and she brought her journalist's knack for notetaking to her new career. The moment she finishes a class, she pulls out a tiny notebook and jots down which lessons worked that day and which ones failed. She then has a resource to refer to when the next term rolls around.

I am constantly looking back at my files, especially after a practice that just kind of fell apart: one where no swimmer did anything well, one where everyone complained the whole time. I'm looking for inspiration from my historical records. So which notepad do I often turn to first? Any one from 2003, a year when Michael was phenomenal in every way. I'll flip through a pad, turning to a page—any page (it doesn't matter; he swam well almost every day)—and see what we did that day. Immediately, my confidence is renewed.

Listen, the road to reaching our ultimate vision can be a long one, the daily grind consuming us. But remember: Each day should present an opportunity to get closer to the vision, not get overwhelmed by it. A daily self-assessment will give you the needed separation from what you've just done and what you still need to do. So here's my suggestion: Take ten minutes at the end of each day. Pop open a

Pellegrino or pour a glass of Merlot or make a cup of hot chocolate. Your call. Just be sure that while you're kicking back, you're also looking at the day's efforts and making an honest assessment of your progress toward your vision. Ideally, it might spur your imagination. You'll imagine, perhaps, three things that you can add to your routine that will help you move closer to success. Write them down, and then think how you can plug them into your process in the coming days.

They will add fuel to your vision drive. They will challenge you to apply a bit more pressure to your effort. They will inspire you to push a little harder tomorrow.

They will eventually make you better overall. And that's one prediction I'm happy to make.

7

RULE 6: A TEAM APPROACH CAN BRING INDIVIDUAL SUCCESS

Often—okay, very often—when I'm introduced to an audience or quoted in a newspaper article, my name comes with an appendage: Bob Bowman, "Michael Phelps's personal coach." It is sort of like how Tonto is always referred to as "the Lone Ranger's sidekick" and Hannibal Hamlin's name is usually followed by "Abraham Lincoln's first vice president."

Now, don't me wrong. My association with the greatest Olympian of all time is eternally flattering and eminently rewarding. It's taken me to the front row of history and brought me to the heights of a sport I love. But I sometimes cringe when I see "personal coach" because in many ways that description masks more than it reveals. Those who don't know the two of us may think that I've been Michael's one and only mentor or confidant over the years or that I've had some Svengali-like hold over him, a Wizard of Ahs pushing buttons that propel him through the water and by competitors and to medal stands and to the riches that come with global stardom.

Oh, if only I had such power.

Yes, over the past two decades Michael and I have had perhaps the closest coach-athlete relationship in sports. I'd say the only one that rivals ours is the pairing of Gregg Popovich and Tim Duncan, which started in 1997, the same year that Michael and I teamed up. (With those two leading the way, the San Antonio Spurs have won five NBA titles.) In our time together, Michael and I have spent thousands of hours on pool decks contemplating racing techniques and training plans, and in airports traveling to competitions, and at press conferences talking to the media, and with manufacturers developing new swimsuits, and at dinner . . . just talking. We've become family.

That said, I know that the success Michael has enjoyed is the product of a team of people, not of a pair of individuals. Early on, when I saw the enormous talent Michael had, I recognized the need to assemble a cadre of advisers and assistants who would help him reach the level he seemed destined for. As such, while Michael may be the most decorated individual Olympic champion of all time, it's the multitude of Team Phelps members who deserve accolades (if not medals) for guiding him to that distinction.

Who composes Team Phelps? Mostly people with whom the public isn't that familiar. It's the doctors and trainers and sports psychologists who work with Michael and with many of my swimmers. It's Rich Wilkens, who started at

Meadowbrook working in the snack bar as a teenager and is now my director of operations, the one who makes sure that if an athlete has to be in Barcelona on May 3 for a meet she's there. It's Cathy Bennett, who taught Michael how to swim even though "he didn't like to get his face wet at first," as she likes to tell people. Today, Cathy directs the Michael Phelps Swim School, which has operations around the world. It's Keenan Robinson, who didn't know a thing about swimming when he first met Michael—Keenan had mostly been training football and baseball players—but became so attuned to the physical toll the sport takes on a swimmer's body that he has dedicated his career to improving swimmers' conditioning. It's Debbie, Michael's mother, and his sisters, Hilary and Whitney, who accompanied him around the world to cheer for him at meets.

In truth, Team Phelps is dozens of other people, too.

Do you see where I'm going? Michael's accomplishments are the result of a collection of "personal coaches."

And that leads me to my next rule: To successfully reach your vision, you will need supporters—friends, family members, coaches, bosses, co-workers, colleagues, teachers. The list could go on and on, or it could be kept to a manageable few, but the point is that you'll come to depend on these people for inspiration, suggestions, advice—and perhaps even for a beer and a burger after a long week of working through the Game Plan. If you have just started a small business, for instance, it's the core group of employees and advisers whom you will lean on as the business advances through the early stages of entrepreneurship. If you're an ultra-marathon runner with the dream of completing a 100-mile race in the heat and the darkness and the exhausted state that such a race demands, it's the pace crew driving alongside you, pitching encouragement (and snacks) as your body starts to wither. If you're a politician seeking office, it's the pack of volunteers stuffing envelopes with campaign flyers and proving to be just as valuable as the consultants you've hired.

Success in most endeavors is the product of a partnership, not the result of acting in isolation. And the beauty of such cooperation is that you get to share your success with those who have aided you. One of my greatest memories during Michael's Olympic career came shortly after he won the 400-meter individual medley in Athens in 2004. He was just nineteen, still really a youngster in many ways and with an innocent streak to prove it. After the race, he told the media, "This is a dream come true. Since I was a little kid, every single day of waking up, hoping to win a gold medal . . . It's everything that I've always wanted to do, and the day is here." Later, at the medal ceremony, he removed the olive wreath from atop his head when "The Star-Spangled Banner" began to play, placing it over his heart as a major leaguer might do with his baseball cap.

He was reveling in the moment, even though he was missing something that was very dear to him.

As soon as the ceremony ended, Michael pulled out his phone and called Hilary, who was still in the stands of the aquatic center where she had watched the race with Debbie and Whitney.

"Meet me at the fence in ten minutes," he told her.

"Okay, the fence."

Debbie asked, "What's going on?"

"That was Michael. He wants us to meet him at the fence."

A few minutes later, Michael and I were standing on one side of a chain-link fence while Debbie, Hilary, and Whitney stood on the other. We were just a couple of hundred feet from the Olympic pool, where thousands of people had watched the competition minutes before. We could just as easily have been in Debbie's backyard; that's how unbothered we were. At that moment no one else was nearby; no one made a fuss over this young swimmer with his first medal.

Michael slipped the medal through the fence. "Mom, look what I did!" he called out.

Debbie teared up as she took hold of the medal. The girls looked over her shoulder. A fence may have separated us, but that piece of gold connected us. At that moment, all the back-and-forth trips Debbie had made to get Michael to practice, all the cheering she and the girls had done at meets, all the training plans I had set up for him, all the miles Michael had swum had finally come together.

Yes, it was Michael's medal, but it was our moment.

No photographers, no TV cameras caught the scene. Simply, this was the start of the journey to eighteen gold medals. We took the moment and hugged it. A victory for Team Phelps.

RULE 6.1: BUILD A SUPPORT TEAM THAT WILL HELP YOU—AS YOU HELP THEM.

Most days during a practice, I walk up and down the length of the pool, observing what my swimmers are doing, keeping on eye on the pace clock, and shouting out instructions above the noise of splashing water. In these moments, the swimmers are just that: swimmers. I don't think of them as among the greatest in the world. I don't consider what they've accomplished in the past or what they may accomplish come the Summer Games in Rio. All I'm thinking is: Will they finish this set strong? Are they hitting today's goals? Are they using the tactics we gave them yesterday?

It's only later, usually when I'm alone and at the end of a busy day, that I reflect on what has come together—this Dream Team of Swimmers. Since the start of this Olympic cycle, I've been coaching, at one time or another, a collection of swimmers with a total of twenty-seven gold medals. (That's the same number of World Series titles the New York Yankees have won over ninety years.) When I think of all this talent in one place, and that place is my place, I sometimes wonder, How did this happen? I did not seek these swimmers out; they sought me out.

But why?

The answer I come up with is this: In developing my swimming program, my goal was never to simply be a factory where some kid could come and try to win an Olympic gold medal. No, I wanted something more. I wanted to create an environment in which success becomes inevitable because of a culture that exudes excellence and is sustained by a core group of people who seek excellence every day. Today, when I read or hear that the North Baltimore Aquatic Club is perhaps the best in the business, I can't help but smile.

And that's because I know how difficult it was to get to this level.

Recall, my vision as a young coach was to work with élite swimmers whose goals included setting records. Right now, I'm at the point where I can say I've claimed my vision. But getting there, over a nearly three-decade stretch, required me to seek out and cultivate a team of people who could support me in the challenge I faced. At times, that meant that I needed to step back and do some soul-searching; I needed to understand what my strengths and weaknesses as a coach, as a manager, and as a business leader were.

As you start to put together a support team for your vision quest, your No. 1 action item should be this: Look at the big picture and ask yourself, "Where can I be better and who can help me get better?" The answer to those simple questions will lead you to people who will help you resolve bigger complications when they arise.

In 2008, when I came back to operate Meadowbrook after the Beijing Olympics, I quickly realized that I couldn't do it alone. There were too many leaks in the system and not enough hours in the day to patch them by myself. My specialty was coaching high-performance swimmers, not reading spreadsheets or mapping out design innovations for the club. So after the first bungled year that I've told you about, the one when we lost so much money and I lost so much mind power, I did an assessment both of the club and of myself. I've already laid out how the club has turned out; that assessment led to the five-year plan that got us back in financial shape.

But I realized that if I was going to continue to be a top-level coach while having the added responsibilities of a business owner, I would need help in the trenches. I knew there would be days when the business and the managerial side of Meadowbrook would pull me away from the pool deck. On those days when I couldn't commit totally to coaching, I had to have backup. I had to have a team of coaches that I could trust with my vision. At first, I brought in several assistants who, at one time or another, had swum for me. They knew my process, they knew my style, and they knew my expectations. They came in, they contributed, they helped build the program—and they did such a good job that they got hired away by other programs.

Was I surprised? No way. When you hire well, and those good people produce, then you can expect that they may get poached. But such turnover means you are constantly trying to fill the ranks, and that can deplete your enthusiasm and cut into your forward progress.

With that in mind, I began to look internally when positions arose, to people who seemed capable of accepting more responsibility—and whose long-term plans included staying close to home. By giving them added responsibilities, I helped them grow as employees and as people and heightened their allegiance to the club and to me. So, for instance, Keenan, whom I had first met when he was fresh out of graduate school, now became even more central to my overall training philosophy. I brought him to national and international meets, and he even began representing the club at swim-related conferences. And there was Gary Peeples, who originally worked at Meadowbrook while in high school. He later went to work at Coca-Cola as a brand manager. I brought him back to head the franchising of the Michael Phelps Swim School around the country. And, more and more, I gave Erik Posegay the chance to plan workouts for the élite swimmers. I wanted my professional swimmers to feel comfortable with my No. 2, especially knowing that I could get pulled away from practice at any time. I also wanted Erik to feel comfortable leading the group, as I saw him as my eventual successor—which he eventually became when I left NBAC to take over the Arizona State program.

When we weren't on the pool deck, my team and I worked side by side in our tiny office space, which allowed us to get to know one another awfully well. We often went on runs or did Insanity workouts together. We pushed one another, a team of professionals helping one another meet our collective and individual goals. It had taken me a while to develop a core team, but when I did the results were worth the wait: I never felt better about the direction in which my vision was heading.

I could not have gotten this far without the help of others.

RULE 6.2: CONNECT WITH PEOPLE WHO WANT TO HELP. THEY'RE OUT THERE.

In 2001, shortly after Michael set his first world record, Debbie, Michael, and I met to once again discuss his future. As I've said, you want to do a reassessment of your Game Plan to make sure your goals continue to align with your overall vision. Well, by becoming the youngest swimmer ever to shatter a world record (he was just fifteen), Michael had accelerated his trajectory; he was moving toward stardom in the sport much faster than I ever imagined.

With that in mind, that fall, when he was just a junior in high school, we made the decision to have him turn professional. A lawyer we knew helped us to negotiate a deal with Speedo. This meant that Michael wouldn't be able to swim in college—the traditional route most top-level swimmers follow—but we could also start investigating other avenues that would allow him to take financial advantage of his growing athletic prominence. Here was the catch: I knew nothing about sponsorships or sports agents or deal-making. I was a swim coach. I needed to find a professional well versed in this area who could make this transition work.

Over several weeks and months, I talked to fellow coaches and asked them for ideas; invariably, any leads failed to hit pay dirt. While swimming is an enormously popular sport among TV viewers during the Games, historically it hasn't produced very many commercially viable athletes. The one that comes to mind is Mark Spitz, who parlayed his seven gold medals in 1972 into sponsorship deals with Kodak and Xerox, among others. As such, my search for someone who could advise Michael through this phase was slow-going.

Then, one morning in the winter of 2002, I turned on the *Today* show. The program was being broadcast live from Salt Lake City, where the Winter Olympics were under way. The guest appearing at that moment was a fellow by the name of Peter Carlisle, a sports agent for many of the Olympic athletics. As he was talking with Matt Lauer, Peter got my attention when he mentioned the possible commercial opportunities that some athletes might earn from a good showing in the Games.

Hmm, I thought. I grabbed a pen and scribbled Peter's name down in my notebook. A Google search and a few phone calls later, Michael and I had an appointment with him.

I tell this story because I think it helps to show a key point: You never know how a relationship with a valuable support person may develop. As such, you need to be open to making new acquaintances, asking friends for referrals, and admitting to others that you could use help in a particular endeavor. In your search for supporters, the last thing you want to be is deferential. In my experience, most people want to help out; they just need to be asked. As a case in point, consider Bart Yasso, one of the most famous runners in the world—even though he's never won an Olympic medal or placed at the Boston Marathon or run a four-minute mile.

If he's not a superstar, you ask, then who is this Bart guy? Well, he is the ultimate cheerleader for recreational runners. He appears at more than fifty races a year, announcing the middle- and back-of-the-pack runners as they cross the finish line. He has more than fifty-five thousand Twitter followers. He is known as the Mayor of Running by those who know him, and that seems to be everyone in the sport. What makes Bart such a compelling figure is that if you are a new runner—say, you're middle-aged and looking to get into shape but haven't put on a pair of running shoes since the Reagan administration—then you contact Bart; he will somehow connect you to a runner in your area who will get you on the course toward your first mile. As Bart likes to tell people, he has the best job in the world. He connects people to a way of life that will help them live an *even* better way of life. Bart is there to help. He's just waiting for a phone call or an email or a tweet.

He is the kind of person who guides people toward their dreams.

Peter Carlisle is just that kind of person, too. Let me get back to his story and I'll show you what I mean.

Our first meeting with Peter got off to a shaky start. When Michael and I arrived at our attorney's office, the staff had prepared a nice lunch spread in a conference room. Michael, never shy around a buffet, filled his plate to overflowing—and then proceeded to drop everything on the floor. Shards of fine china scattered everywhere.

Peter didn't flinch. "Let me help you," he said to Michael.

I just chuckled. "Are you sure you're ready for this?" I asked him.

Peter simply said, "No worries."

But it wasn't Peter's easygoing nature that won Michael and me over. Throughout the hour or so we spent together that afternoon, I never heard Peter push an agenda on us or bring up the megadollars Michael could potentially earn. Instead, he patiently listened to Michael as he discussed his career, the goals he had in the pool, the records he hoped to set. Peter could see that Michael had a vision that was performance-based, which was fine, but he kept prodding. He wanted Michael, it seemed, to set out a vision that was personality-based. Finally, Peter asked, "Michael, what is your goal for the long term? What do you see yourself accomplishing beyond the records and the medals?"

Michael paused for a second. He looked at me. He

rubbed his chin. Finally, he looked at Peter and said, "I want to change the sport of swimming."

Since that meeting fourteen years ago, Peter and his colleagues have made Michael one of the top sports marketing personalities in the world. Michael's roster of endorsement deals runs longer than his six-foot-four-inch frame. As a result of the work Peter and his team have done, Michael lives a very comfortable life. But beyond the dollars Peter ultimately secured, the lynchpin of our arrangement was Peter's desire to connect with Michael's long-term goal. And here he succeeded as well. Through the Michael Phelps Foundation—which got its initial funding thanks to a sponsorship deal Peter negotiated—Michael is bringing the sport of swimming to children around the world. Each month he does a number of talks for youth groups, sharing the story of exercise and water safety and the fun of being in the water.

It is one of the jobs Michael will have when he finally finishes his swimming career. And it is due to his partnership with Peter, who saw a vision and not just a transaction.

RULE 6.3: FIND THE "LIKE-MINDED" TO PULL YOU THROUGH THE TOUGHEST MOMENTS.

One day before practice, Tom Luchsinger tweeted the following:

You know you're tired when you walk into the office, look at the conference table and think to yourself, "Damn, that looks comfortable!"

As I've told you, Tom was a model citizen from the moment he joined my program. Mr. Perfect, remember? He rarely missed a practice, even when the workouts weren't leading to the best results in competitions. I don't think I ever heard him complain. That tweet may be the closest admission to fatigue (and frustration) I picked up from Tom during our time together.

Honestly, I couldn't blame him or any of his fellow swimmers if they expressed weariness now and then. They've taken on a very challenging pursuit. Trying to make an Olympic team takes a deep reserve of stamina and mental strength. Imagine exerting four years of work and effort without knowing that the reward you crave is a certainty. And the pursuit is *always* in front of them. My swimmers are constantly reminded of their goal: I remind them, the photos of past Olympians on our walls remind them, and the mere presence of their fellow athletes reminds them. Being enmeshed in such a mission can easily lead to bouts of exhaustion and unease. The excitement of starting a new adventure has dissolved in their rearview mirrors, while the finish line they desire is still thousands of miles away.

It's at times like these that having support people nearby becomes critical—especially people who can appreciate the difficulties you're facing.

Fortunately, my swimmers have found that. "We have a certain set of goals that attract other swimmers," Matt McLean said one day of his fellow swimmers. "We are like-minded."

Anyone pursuing a long-term dream will eventually hit a wall. The chase is long and it can eat you up. When that happens, you must look for help from the "like-minded." People who can appreciate the challenges you're enduring. If you are a Ph.D. student, for example, and facing five to six years of studies and research and dissertation defending, your road will be much smoother if you connect with other doctoral students. Or maybe you have plans to take a trip—a very long trip. Say, like the trip Scott Kelly took off on in March 2015. Traveling with two cosmonauts to the International Space Station, Kelly knew fame awaited him; upon his return, he would become the first American to have spent a year in space. But that also meant that he would be apart from his Earth-bound family and friends and the other things he loved. As he told the media before his trip, he expected to miss "the rain, the breeze, the change of seasons." Simple pleasures, to be sure. But he also offered what would get him through the mission: his support team. "I couldn't ask for a better two professional cosmonauts to fly with," Kelly said. "We are all great friends."

I don't think anybody achieves anything as an individual. You're always going to need support from someone else. Whatever you pursue, you don't want to attempt to go it alone.

My guys found connections through their individual pursuits. Many nights after a practice, they would go to a movie or make dinner together. Often a few of them, including Allison and Jessica, would spend time at a local children's program inspiring the kids with their medals and their stories. By teaming up, they pulled one another through the rough spots. As Tom said one day, "Swimming is an individual sport, but you can make it team-oriented. As hard as a workout can be, we all enjoy coming to work out every day and pushing each other and pushing ourselves."

And leaning on one another, too.

RULE 6.4: AVOID THOSE PEOPLE WHO WILL PULL YOU DOWN.

In many ways, my team of Olympic hopefuls came together very surreptitiously. An unexpected tweet from Yannick brought him to Baltimore. My chance meeting with Jessica in Boston led her to Meadowbrook. Lotte's interest in seeing how Americans trained inspired her move from Denmark. Along with the other professionals working with me, these swimmers came with exceptional swimming talent and skills.

And they shared one more thing: personalities perfectly suited to my vision.

How do I know? Because none of them failed what I call the Knucklehead Exam.

Understand, if you are a knucklehead, you're not welcome by those on a vision quest.

What's a knucklehead? In my world, it is someone who doesn't buy into our system or won't follow our rules or doesn't value the same things we do. We believe very strongly in coming to practice, giving your best effort, pushing past your limit, and trying to be better today than you were yesterday. In other words, doing more than squeaking by.

To be part of our team you also must respect your teammates, support your teammates, know how to treat your teammates. Essentially, your behavior is as important to me as your talent.

Listen, I'm looking for people who want to succeed on the top level but can also help others reach that level. People who enjoy working together. They like the fact that there is a competitive environment in play every day—and they will encourage the swimmer in the lane next to them to do better, work harder, be stronger.

Allison Schmitt provided a good insider's take on what it means to work within such an environment. During one of the first practices, when all the Olympians and potential Olympians were in the water, Schmitty took a break and looked around. Stars in every lane, each pushing the one in front to keep going forward. She then spotted Michael in the next lane over. "Michael," she shouted, "I feel like I'm in Olympic training camp right now. This is crazy. These guys know how to work *and* have fun."

Yes, when people with a purpose come together, and pull together, things can be fun.

And when they don't . . .

Through the years, I've made my share of mistakes; I've accepted swimmers into the program who turned out to be knuckleheads—and their presence threatened to steal energy from the collective and instill negativity in our routine. Here's a perfect example: In 2009, shortly after I had moved back to Baltimore from the University of Michigan, I was working with some recent college graduates who wanted to invest one more cycle toward making the next Olympic team. One of the swimmers—I'll call him Roger, so as to save him from further embarrassment—was probably one of the top three or four swimmers in his event. He certainly had a chance to make the 2012 U.S. team. But when I agreed to let him swim with our group I only knew of his past performance in the pool, not his personality.

After a couple of months of practice, it became apparent that Roger was a knucklehead who wasn't ready to apply our practice principles to his Olympic mission. He also had a blasé attitude and wasn't game for taking too much constructive input. During one practice, I offered him a tip that I thought might improve his stroke. I was acting as the coach that I am. But, as I walked away, Roger muttered to Michael, "It don't matter."

Later, MP told me about the line, and I became incensed.

"What does he mean, 'It don't matter'?" I barked. "Every little thing matters if you want to be better than just good." My anger intensified with each word out of my mouth. Michael got a chuckle out of that, and for weeks afterward, just to irritate me, he would snicker as he walked by me, "It don't matter."

The fact is, it *does* matter: How you practice the little things. How you take to advice. How you work with teammates. How you inspire others. It *all* matters.

Pursuing your vision, as I've mentioned, involves working your daily Game Plan and seeking to achieve small goals on the way to the dream goal. It is a series of small steps. With each one, though, the difficulty often increases. You will need the support of others to lift you up—but not if "the other" offers an attitude of "It don't matter."

Eventually, I asked Roger to leave the program, but I didn't forget him. After we wrap up a great workout or when I notice one of my swimmers helping out a teammate or when someone nails a time that he's never hit before, I send out a complimentary tweet that includes the hashtag *#itdoesmatter*. The hashtag has become another reminder of what we need to do in order to reach our goals—and that includes choosing our support team wisely.

We all feed off the inspiration others provide, the enthusiasm they show, the pitch-perfect personalities they display.

RULE 6.5: HELP OTHERS BELIEVE IN THEMSELVES.

Over the years, I've become a great fan of Ken Burns and the documentaries he has produced. All you need to do is watch the *Civil War* or *Baseball* or *Lincoln* series to realize how he has elevated the documentary to an artistic form. But, of all his works, one film resonates with me more than any other.

It's the one Burns did on the famed architect Frank Lloyd Wright. I didn't know much about Wright until I tuned in. Burns provides all the essential layers to Wright's magnificent career, but what stuck with me was something Burns shares early in the biography. We learn that Wright dropped out of college and moved from his home in Milwaukee to Chicago with barely a possession to his name. And yet he seemed to have no worries. Why? Because before Wright left home his mother told him not to worry about his future; she believed he could do something great.

Belief. I contend that that is one of the greatest gifts you can share with others: the belief that they can succeed.

Like Mrs. Wright, that's what my parents gave me.

While my mom and dad were relatively successful people, they were hardly tycoons or folks whose names regularly appeared in bold-faced type in the society section of our local South Carolina newspaper. My mother was a schoolteacher. My father was an administrator at a state agency. They did their jobs, and did them very well—and they expected my sister and me to follow a similar path. If we did, they told us, we would do just fine out in the world.

From their grounding I got my focus, and the mind-set that how you do things is as important as what happens when they're done. And I supplemented my parents' examples with those of people I met along the way. For instance, at one point I had a very good violin teacher, Dr. John Bauer, who was a concertmaster for the South

Carolina Philharmonic Orchestra. Working with him, seeing his approach to music and teaching, listening as he made notes and scales understandable, I started to value the quality not only of the music but also of the instruction. I began to believe that you *can* affect others—and how you do that can help bring someone's dream closer to reality.

As you go after your big-dream vision, look for people who will not only help you but also believe in you. People who want you to succeed and will provide you with the support and the feedback you might need. People—a boss, a mentor, a close friend—who will bring a healthy dose of honesty to the process. Going into sales? Then look for a sales director who has a reputation for stating clearly what it takes to amend a faulty sales strategy. Want to join a major symphony orchestra? Then don't be satisfied if your violin instructor offers an easy "Good job!" when the reality is that you're missing most of your chords.

Look for the three In's: Instruction. Inspiration. Involvement.

As I said earlier, I'm very fortunate to have teamed up with Michael and to have been a part of an amazing journey. I know that I've taught him much about the tactical side of swimming. But, just as important, I feel that I've been there for him when challenges outside the pool have tested his strength and disposition. When he has stumbled, he has known that he could reach out to me.

Yes, he could reach out to his personal coach.

8

RULE 7: STAY MOTIVATED
OVER THE LONG HAUL

One of my all-time favorite sports memories came shortly after Michael won his eighth gold medal in Beijing, the medal that broke Mark Spitz's record for most golds at a single Olympic Games. Once the formal press conference was over, several NBC press people grabbed Michael and me, rushed us into a golf cart waiting outside the Water Cube, and drove us to NBC Sports headquarters.

"Drove" may actually be too strong of a way to put it. Let's try *waddled* instead.

That's because hundreds of cheering, raucous Chinese fans clogged the streets around the Water Cube, all of them wanting to get up close and personal with the new Olympic king. In the process, they kept our cart from revving beyond four miles per hour.

When we finally arrived at the NBC center, the media people directed us deep into the complex and to the front door of Dick Ebersol's office, which also doubled as his apartment during the Games. Dick's connection with the Olympics dates from the late 1960s, when he was a young researcher for ABC Sports. Eventually, he moved to NBC and became president of the sports division. He oversaw every Winter and Summer Olympics broadcast from 1992 through the 2008 Games. He lived, breathed, and slept the Olympics, a fact duly noted by the sign above his door, which read SLEEPING. If it was turned off, you could go in. If it was illuminated, you didn't dare.

Fortunately, when we arrived Dick was very much awake.

I'll never forget Dick's reaction when he saw Michael. He rushed over and bear-hugged him—and who could blame him? Dick had convinced the Olympic organizers to move the finals of the swimming events to the morning hours in Beijing. That way, NBC could show the events live and in prime time back in the U.S. Obviously, with the huge ratings NBC earned thanks to Michael's historic eight-gold run, Dick was ecstatic.

But business and profits weren't the motives behind Dick's affection. In 2004, Dick had lost a son, Teddy, in a terrible plane crash; in the years that had followed, he had become a mentor to Michael. In no way was Michael a surrogate for Teddy, but he and Dick had shared many meaningful conversations during the time Michael was developing into a sports celebrity.

Now, here, in an out-of-the-way office somewhere in

Beijing, I was witnessing a touching scene: one of the sports world's most decorated athletes and one of its most powerful executives in a true embrace.

Dick invited us to take a seat on his living-room couch, just in front of a huge, multi-screen board where he could watch every event being televised. He then hit a button that launched a four-minute video tribute to that year's Olympians; the segment had aired on the first night of NBC's coverage. Michael and I hadn't yet seen it. We started watching; it was a beautiful, compelling video. We chuckled when we spotted Michael in a scene. Midway through, I turned to Dick and saw a couple of tears dripping from his eyes. He looked at me and said, "Every time I see this I cry. And I've probably seen it hundreds of times!"

Right then I realized how much this man loved what he did. Yes, he was in a high-pressure position. Yes, his network had huge dollars at stake—and many of those dollars were based on decisions he needed to make. Yes, the days and nights during the Games were long, tense, and often sleepless ones.

And yet for all the challenges and pressure, Dick Ebersol still maintained the same passion for the Olympics that he had when the Games originally lured him into the TV sports business forty years earlier.

In the pursuit of your goals and your dream vision, one critical ingredient you'll need is passion—that intense interest or affection that starts to develop once you hit upon something you're drawn to. Passion often separates the high-level achievers from the mere dreamers. For instance, consider what distinguishes the best schoolteachers from the back-of-the-pack ones. Over the years, I've talked to a number of teachers (remember, my mom was one), and I often ask them why they stay in the profession, with all the bureaucracy and the long hours and the endless grading and the paltry pay scale. All too often, the best ones tell me, it's for the joy they get out of inspiring young minds. That's what fuels their passion. Similarly, I ask the sports writers I've gotten to know why they stay in journalism at a time when the profession is going through so much turmoil and with so many of their colleagues getting laid off. Inevitably, their answer is: "We love covering sports. Every day there's a new story to write." That's what fuels their passion.

But even people who love their jobs and their pursuits—even schoolteachers, sports writers, and professional swimmers—face days when the motivation to execute the Game Plan *once more* lags, or isn't there at all. Something is getting in the way; perhaps it's some type of adversity, or it may simply be the routine of the pursuit, the burnout effect, taking hold. And, as a result, the normal attention and energy they devote to the pursuit wanes.

To help you get through the dog-day moments when they crop up during your vision quest, let me offer some of the strategies I've used with my swimmers. I'll also reveal the secrets I've applied when my own passion dips. (Understand something: The fact that you're coaching or managing or mentoring someone doesn't mean that you're immune to the "dog days.") Passion for a particular pursuit is critical, but, as with anything we love, we need to find ways to keep our interest kindled. Having such triggers will allow you to pursue excellence even on the days when you don't feel so excellent.

RULE 7.1: ON THE DARK DAYS, CONVINCE YOURSELF TO STAY IN FOCUS.

Michael Phelps and Allison Schmitt have a good bit in common. The two have been teammates for more than a decade; they started swimming together on a club team I coached in the mid-2000s while I was also the coach at the University of Michigan. Both have made multiple Olympic teams, and between them they've collected twenty-eight Olympic medals. By now, they're so familiar with each other that you might mistake them for brother and sister, especially when the teasing and the ribbing kick in.

That said, one thing that distinguishes the two is their mood first thing in the morning. As I've mentioned before, when Michael arrives for a 7 A.M. practice he comes with half-opened eyes and a scowl that says, "Approach with caution." Over the years, I've learned to save my "Good morning" until after he's done his warm-up swim. Schmitty, on the other hand, shows up with the cheerfulness of a TV weatherperson—all upbeat, talkative, smiling. She's that way even though the sun is barely up, a chill may be in the air, and a muscle-testing, exhausting 7,000 meters of swimming awaits her. For the next sixty to ninety minutes she will, like a metronome, swim the length of the pool and back many times, following the lane's ubiquitous black line, a black line that she has stared at hundreds of times in the years of working out. And when she's done she knows what's coming later in the day: 7,000 more meters, and more time staring at the black line.

And you think your job gets monotonous.

Yet every morning there's All-In Allison—No-Complaining Schmitty—with that beautiful smile. How does she not let the *sameness* get to her?

After one of our practices during the summer of 2014, about a year into our training for Rio, Allison spoke with a reporter who was visiting Meadowbrook that day—and she admitted that the repetition and the routine and the work does get to her at times. "Yes, there are days when you don't want to go to practice, but there are days when *most* people don't want to go to work," she told the reporter. When he asked her if she had a secret for combating those bad days, she nodded. "I get by with a fake-it-till-you-make-it attitude." *What's that mean?* he asked. "Eventually, if you tell yourself enough that it will be fun getting in the water," Allison replied, "you'll trick yourself into being happy even when you don't want to."

In many respects, Schmitty was right on target.

Some days you just have *to work* at going to work, especially if you're ultimately pursuing a bigger prize. Regardless of your mood, you must stay committed to your Game Plan and your daily goals. I know it's not easy, but I also know that it's essential. Admittedly, I don't always feel like running down to the pool deck and coaching Olympic gold medalists. Trust me, plenty of days come along when I'd rather be doing a hundred other things: heading out to Pimlico Race Course in time for the day's first race; walking along the Delaware shoreline at sunrise with a caffe latte from Starbucks. And when those days crop up I, like Schmitty, must "fake" my interest until the spark reignites the fire. Through the years, I've learned something: It always does.

One trick that helps me snap back into focus is to look at an app on my iPhone that counts down the days left until Rio. As you recall, the number started at 1,068 when we launched our training in September 2013. Like the seconds ticking off the clock in Times Square on New Year's Eve, the number on my app keeps getting smaller: 976 . . . 628 . . . 421 . . . 188 . . .

"Pretty soon, Bob," I'll say to myself on those days when I need a kick, "zero will be here. Let's get to work. Show these swimmers that you're as motivated as they are."

Why "sell" such energy? Because over the years I've also learned that my swimmers feed off that emotion, that passion—especially on days when they may be struggling for motivation. Again, I'll let Allison explain the effect: "You can use other people's energies to help goose you up or get you through the rough spot. This team is very good about pushing one another. If they see someone that's down, then they're going to help that person figure it out."

Everyone is going to have tough days en route to the dream goal. The trick is to have a stimulus ready that will push you past the blockades and keep you on track.

7.2: MAKE EVERY DAY SEEM NOT LIKE EVERY DAY.

Earlier, I mentioned my appreciation for the way Michigan football coach Jim Harbaugh does his job—for the way his brand of self-discipline and daily goal-setting have inspired his teams to go from out of contention to ahead of the pack. But although I'm a big fan of Jim's, I root even harder for his older brother, John Harbaugh. Here's why: John coaches my team, the Baltimore Ravens.

In a way, John's career in Baltimore mirrors my second stint in the city. John took over the Ravens in 2008, just about the same time that I was returning to Baltimore from my four years coaching at the University of Michigan. At that point, the Ravens had hit a rough patch; it had been eight years since the team last won a Super Bowl. But by the end of John's first season, the Ravens had become a dominant, competitive club built around a crushing defense and a fairly reliable offense. The team's maturation under Harbaugh peaked in 2012—the same year Michael was capturing his title as Olympic king. The Ravens finished the regular season with a 10–6 record, moved through the early rounds of the playoffs, and won the team's second

Super Bowl, beating the San Francisco 49ers (coached by Jim Harbaugh at the time).

In addition to winning a Super Bowl title, John has distinguished himself in another way: He is the only NFL coach to win playoff games in six of his first seven seasons in the league. What's his secret to being so consistently competitive? Sure, like his brother, John knows the game's X's and O's. But he is also recognized as a master of keeping his players excited about coming to work every day. The football season is a long one: six weeks of training camp, sixteen weeks with games, and, if you're lucky, several more weeks of playoff action. It's bruising, both to the body and to the mind. And with that kind of grueling and repetitive schedule it's easy for a "kids' game" to morph into physical, emotional drudgery.

To his credit, Harbaugh doesn't let that happen. He continually devises different schemes that prevent the season from becoming routine. For instance, he will often bring in guest speakers from the business and entertainment worlds to talk to his players. The sessions may have nothing to do with football, but they engage the players and get them thinking beyond the confines of a 100-yard field. He'll even ask his own players to present on occasion. One time during the 2012 training camp, Harbaugh had the guard Marshal Yanda address the squad. The summer's heat had threatened to sap the players' drive. Yanda told his teammates that under these conditions they needed to "embrace the grind" and not be defeated by it. Harbaugh took to Yanda's message; days later, he presented his players with "Embrace the Grind" T-shirts. The coach has also taken players on field trips. During training camp in 2013, he canceled practice one day and rounded up a group of rookies for a trip to Gettysburg, Pennsylvania. The players and the coach spent several hours touring the area's noted battlefields. A history lesson rather than a training session, for sure, but productive just the same.

The talks, the T-shirts, the trips: Do these diversions make the players better prepared to beat their opponents come Sunday? Apparently so. From 2008 to 2014, Harbaugh's teams had the second most victories among NFL teams. If anything, these schemes have helped his players stay motivated and fresh throughout a challenging (and long) season.

I've tried to incorporate similar tactics into my program; as a former competitive swimmer, I know that the routine of the sport can wear on the spirit as much as it does on the body. In the years prior to the London Games, when Michael was having trouble getting motivated for another Olympic run, I introduced Friends Friday; the swimmers could bring a buddy to work out with them. Michael invited a range of friends, including members of the Ravens. When these stars showed up, everyone at the pool—including me—got pumped up. We also have theme parties for the team. During the 2014 summer, we celebrated with a "Half-Way to Rio Roast," a night to highlight how far we had come toward meeting our Olympic vision (and to chow down on some delicious Maryland pit beef). And when I used to coach very young swimmers—the ones still in grade school and high school—I would sometimes have a thirty-minute storytelling session before a weekend practice. The kids would share something they learned at school that week. Again, it was something to break up the routine while letting the kids get to know their teammates a little better.

Such motivational tactics are hardly revolutionary. Companies from Apple to Yahoo! are regularly touted for operating workplaces with morale-boosting strategies. They know the tactics work, and so do I. My recommendation: The more you can sprinkle motivational practices into the regular vision quest, the easier it will be to keep the passion for the vision charged up. Need added proof? Let me quote Marshal Yanda of "Embrace the Grind" fame. After the Ravens won the Super Bowl following the 2012 season, he told reporters, "A Super Bowl is a great goal, but it can't be why you play this game. It has to be for your love of the game and for the guy lined up next to you. In the end, it's about the competitiveness, the work you put in, and because you love it."

RULE 7.3: FIND ANOTHER PASSION TO OFFSET THE GRIND THAT COMES WITH YOUR PRIMARY ONE.

The Grind. Marshal Yanda used those words when addressing his Ravens teammates. John Harbaugh had them printed on the T-shirts he gave to his players. It seems I'm hearing that phrase a lot these days. Funny, I don't remember my mom or dad coming home from work and complaining about "the grind." In fact, when their workdays ended, they ended. Mom and Dad knew how to restrict talk of work to a certain portion of their lives. Our dinner conversations revolved around sports, music, food, school, current events; not Mom's lesson plans for tomorrow or Dad's presentation at the next administrators' meeting.

But today everyone seems to be "grinding" through his or her work weeks. How come? Maybe technology is to blame. With our smartphones and laptops and iPads, we can't get away from work; we're "on call" all the time, and that means we're always grinding. I know the drill. As I've told you, I'm up by 4:30 A.M. each day, but by 5 A.M., while I'm fixing breakfast, I'm also reading emails, checking sports news on ESPN.com, and Googling "motivational quotes" to find some words of wisdom to tweet to my swimmers. The birds aren't even chirping yet, and I've tap-danced across the keyboard of my iPhone a dozen times already.

I don't think you can put all the blame on technology, though. In fact, sometimes I feel as if I've been grinding—working very hard—for much of my life. When I look back at my college years, I sometimes wonder if I even went to school. I started coaching in my junior year, and I was so driven to become a better coach that I would be at the pool by 6 A.M. and not leave until 8 P.M. Even after I had left Florida State, I kept up that routine at the different swim programs where I coached. Work was my livelihood and my hobby. I loved what I was doing and wanted to do as much as—or even more than—I could. My passion propelled me around the country, to new coaching opportunities and to new places where I could improve my craft.

But after about a decade of coaching I began to realize that I was becoming a one-trick pony. That swimming dominated my life. So what did I do? I turned to the ponies.

Here's the deal: In 1996, I was working with Paul Bergen, the legendary coach whose brain I was always trying to pick. On the side, Paul owned some thoroughbreds, so I began to accompany him to his barn, ostensibly to tease out more swimming insights. But the more I visited his barn the more I became interested in the horses and in horse racing. I began to do what I usually do: I immersed myself in the sport. Every book on horse training and breeding that I could find, I read. Every video available, I watched. Over time, I fell in love with the pace of the thoroughbred's life, which oddly mimicked my own. There was a rhythm to a horse's training that I could relate to; horses and I shared a similar early-rising lifestyle. And, being around the horses and the smell of the hay and the barn, I was reminded of the summer days that I spent on my grandparents' farm in South Carolina. In time, my newfound interest in thoroughbreds led me to buy horses of my own.

But, mostly, what the horses did was make me a better

swim coach. They provided me with a diversion from my No. 1 passion; I wasn't always thinking about swimming, or overthinking about swimming. They gave me balance.

As you pursue your dream vision, here are some words of caution: Don't let the vision become so important that you neglect other interests or fail to develop new ones. These "secondary" skills can provide much needed perspective. I've told you that Michael Phelps is the most focused person I know; when he's near a pool training or competing, his concentration level is off the charts. But once he's away from the water he knows how to click off and turn to something else. This may take the form of a round of golf or a video game or a card game. Or Michael may just go off to a quiet spot where he can be alone. His mother, Debbie, says that he can find joy by simply sitting in a chair, eyes staring ahead, thinking. "He's actually rather deep," she told me once.

Regardless of the method of choice, MP lets distance from his passion recharge his passion—and so should you.

RULE 7.4: KNOW WHAT MOTIVATES PEOPLE BEYOND THEIR DREAM VISION.

Speaking of Debbie, she came by for dinner one night not long after Michael returned to training. I hadn't seen her in some time, so with a friend of mine we went to one of our favorite spots near Meadowbrook, Crêpe du Jour, and settled in for a nice, long catch-up.

Once the wine had been served and the crêpes came, the

stories bubbled up. At one point, midway through dinner, Debbie shared the following with my friend: "One thing I love about Bob is that as he and Michael grew closer, I realized how much he encompassed every aspect of a kid's life—from sports to school to the kid's physical and emotional well-being. Bob's philosophy was very well rounded. He didn't try to parent a child, but he also wasn't just the swim coach. Not that he would pry into their lives, but he did become part of their world. I think that when you're working with people, to gain their respect you have to have that sense of interest. Bob was interested in everyone in his practice. I parallel it to the classroom. When you're teaching thirty kids in the classroom, you can't teach the same way. It has to be individualized."

I have to say, I was a bit embarrassed by Debbie's words, but I also wouldn't disagree with them. People are emotional beings, and part of helping someone achieve a vision is understanding what motivates the person, what moves the person. Now, does this mean that I'm looking to become best friends with my swimmers? Not at all. I don't want the lines between coach and athlete to blur so much that I can't provide honest, unvarnished feedback. And while Michael and I now have a very close relationship—one that I would certainly describe as a friendship—it did not form until we had spent years being around each other and helping each other in ways beyond swimming.

So while I'm not going to have my swimmers over for a

weekly barbecue, I do look for ways to connect with them and to discover what makes them tick. With such insight, I think I can help them grow both as individuals and as athletes—and give them the motivation to come to practice for more than just a challenging workout. For instance, I know that Tom Luchsinger is a history buff; he could often be seen around the pool deck carrying a biography of John F. Kennedy. Matt McLean likes to restore old cars. Jessica Long is developing a side career as a model. And then there's Yannick Agnel, a swimmer whose talent in the pool is matched only by his curiosity out of it.

Yannick once explained to someone that he left France to train with me in Baltimore because he had "only known one way of coaching in my whole life. I would like to experience this kind of process with someone else. Everybody has his own personality, but something that's really important to me is being balanced in life, and when you're swimming, when you're practicing for six to eight hours a day, it's really, really hard to find a balance. Bob is definitely focused on making you grow up as a man and become more than just a swimmer."

As it turned out, Yannick spent only one year with me; he returned to France after the 2014 season. But during the time that we were together I believe he did develop in ways not reflected just in his freestyle times. He and I would talk about movies, literature, the sights of Paris—the fine life. While he was in the U.S., he made a point of visiting the museums and historical monuments of nearby Washington, D.C. He even took online courses. Though quiet by nature, Yannick exuded a sense of charged wonder.

I look forward to seeing Yannick again in Rio, where he could very likely race against Michael. I will again marvel at his talent, both in and out of the water.

RULE 7.5: INSPIRE WITH IMMEDIATE, NOT DELAYED, FEEDBACK.

Want to keep the passion burning? Here's a great trick: Limit the number of meetings you hold and the number of meetings you attend.

In my experience, gathering a group of people for a regularly scheduled meeting—the "Monday-morning-10-A.M.-what's-ahead-this-week meeting," for instance—quite often zaps people's motivation, instead of sparking it. Yes, I know the potential value of these types of gatherings; information can be shared and ideas might blossom. But experience has shown me that these meetings often lack purpose; all they do is take people out of work mode and into standby mode.

I'll give you an example. In the summer of 2013, I coached the USA men's team that competed at the World Championships in Barcelona. My bosses at USA Swimming told me that I needed to have a team meeting every day, a meeting in which I would talk about the day's events: who was swimming, what time the bus was heading to the aquatic center—information that I could just as easily have shared via email or text. After our first meeting, when the guys barely listened and spent most of the time checking their iPhones, I realized that they didn't need to hear a to-do list at that point in the day. Those twenty minutes could be used for resting or reading or just being left alone with their thoughts.

So I voiced my concern to my bosses, and was told, "Have the daily meeting."

My solution? As directed, we met every day at 3:45 P.M.—and were finished by 3:48 P.M., to a rousing cheer from the swimmers. Talk about motivation. I'm not sure if the shortened sessions had any effect on their performance, but the American men won fifteen medals during that meet, a total well ahead of any other country's.

Now, again, I understand the value of a meeting as a venue for providing employees with a strategic, comprehensive plan. The meeting I had to kick off our Rio training fits that description. It was special, and because I rarely have meetings it conveyed an added sense of urgency. But for routine feedback don't wait for the Monday staff meeting or for a formal "let's go over your strengths and weaknesses" meeting. Give it right away, on the spot. I've learned that the best way to get somebody to improve or to reinforce good behavior or to extinguish bad behavior is in the trenches. Every hour of practice, as I walk up and down the pool deck, I'm giving feedback. I'm also showing my swimmers that I care about them and their effort. Later, if they want to meet privately and talk more on a topic, I'm open to it. But if I can convey my interest in their effort at a moment's notice, and not at a mandatory meeting, they will stay sharp (and so will I).

RULE 7.6: LET YOUR PASSION LEAD YOU, NOT GET AWAY FROM YOU.

I've just told you the motivational value of giving instantaneous feedback. Well, now I'm going to show you how *not* to deliver such feedback. Hopefully, you'll learn a lesson from this story; I certainly did.

Let me set the scene: A June day in 2000. A Baltimore scorcher—ninety-eight degrees, one hundred percent humidity. It's 4 P.M. Hundreds of kids and adults are using the Meadowbrook outdoor pool to cool off. It's loud, with all the little kids screaming and goofing around in the water. Michael and my group are using the indoor pool for a hard practice. I'm bothered by the heat, the noise, and the schedule. In one month, Michael is slated to swim in his first Olympic Trials. If he does well there, he's going to the Olympics.

But on this day Mr. Focus decides to test my patience.

He's not following my workout plan as he normally does. Instead, he's messing around with his buddies; okay, he's acting the way a fifteen-year-old should on a hot summer day. But I won't have any of it. After he finishes one more lackadaisical lap, I go down to the end of the pool. I tell him, "Get out this second!" Everyone at Meadowbrook can hear me, or so I think. But I don't care. I launch into him. "You have to do what I tell you! You're going to work harder, and you're going to listen to me!"

Michael isn't listening; in fact, he starts talking back. That I won't have. "Be quiet!" I tell him. "And do what I say!"

This time he starts walking away, shouting, "I'm getting out of here!"

I say, "Oh, no you're not!"

For the next minute, we're cussing at each other, a thirty-five-year-old hotheaded coach and a fifteen-year-old kid who just wants to have some fun on a hot summer day. Pairs of eyes—hundreds of them—are staring at the two of us. I've created a bad scene. Finally, I say, "Get the hell out of here!" Michael heads off to the locker room.

I'm there on the pool deck. I look around. Meadowbrook is packed with people, but I feel all alone.

Needless to say, this was not one of my finer moments.

I'd like to say that it was the last time I ever yelled at Michael or at any of my swimmers. Safe to say, it wasn't. But as the years have passed and I've matured both as a coach and as a person, that incident has remained vivid in my mind, and informed how I manage and motivate people.

I've learned that motivating people is an art, not a science. You cannot inspire people through intimidation; instead, you need to understand the buttons that must be pushed. Strangely, my revelation has come in part by following the management style of Bob Baffert, the legendary horse trainer. Over the past twenty years, Baffert has been one of the most successful trainers in his sport, capping his record in 2015 when he became the first trainer in thirty-seven years to win the Triple Crown. But while he may not win the Kentucky Derby or the Preakness or the Belmont every year, he always seems to have a horse in the race. How come?

I believe it's because Baffert brings a special perspective to his line of work, a perspective that can be used in any profession, in any process. Too many trainers never let up on their charges, employing an extreme level of intensity each day and demanding daily improvement. Such intensity is unsustainable and, ultimately, unproductive. Baffert, on the other hand, approaches the business with a steely level-headedness. A self-assuredness built upon his experience and the insight he has into those he works with, both man and beast. I'm sure Baffert demands excellence of his people. Yet his approach to reaching such a standard doesn't seem to supersede the long-term goal.

I've come to see the power of Baffert's ways. As a young coach, I used the hammer for every nail that popped up, often to the detriment of my swimmers. Yes, I want my swimmers to approach every practice with this mind-set: *Today's effort will be better than yesterday's.* I do want them to feel that they're doing something important when they enter the water. That the one or two hours of practice will have a payoff. That said, I don't want them to feel that failure—the inevitable lapse that comes with the pursuit of a goal—will nullify the chance to achieve what they want.

That's just too much pressure, and it's pressure that will ultimately harm their growth. It depletes, rather than inspires, their passion.

Have I gone soft? Maybe a little. But I think I've also gotten smarter. I now look to discover what the athlete needs in order to stay passionate, stay charged up—and what can be done to solve problems that develop, not exacerbate them. I feel that I'm a better coach, and motivator, because of this change. My swimmers seem to have noticed. One day not long ago, Allison was asked if I had changed during the ten years that we've worked together. Before answering, she paused, as if waiting for the right words to reach her lips. "It's funny," she finally said. "He's not as loud as he was, and because of that I think he's better. He's mellowed, but in a good way."

9

RULE 8: ADVERSITY
WILL MAKE YOU STRONGER

As we now know, the London Olympics ended on an incredibly high note for Michael Phelps. With three American teammates, he won the 4 x 100-meter medley relay on the last day of competition. At the time, we thought it was his final race ever—and what an awfully nice way to go out. A gold medal. In some ways, it equated to Derek Jeter ending his career with a game-winning hit or to Ray Lewis winning a Super Bowl in his final NFL game. Michael had one more gold, further securing his place in Olympic history. The perfect ending.

But seven nights earlier the picture was anything but ideal.

That was the evening that Michael finished fourth in the 400-meter individual medley, marking the first time since 2000 that he had swum an Olympic event and not medaled. And, with his poor performance coming on the very first day of competition, the whispers began: *Maybe Michael Phelps is done.*

"That was horrible," he said to me moments after the race.

I simply said, "Yes, it was."

I could tell the results really bothered him. He was embarrassed. He'd never had a bad swim at the Olympics, ever. "He's going to have to get over this," I said to myself. I knew that I had to get him reengaged. I began pointing out some technical things he needed to work on, some things he had to practice with his breaststroke because he would need them for the 200-meter individual medley that would be coming up within days. I had barely said a word, though, when Michael launched into me: "I know, I know! I didn't train! I played golf. I didn't come to the pool enough. I can't swim. I know. What else can I do wrong?"

I just said, "You know what, Michael? There's a whole long list of things you've done wrong, but we're going to start with breaststroke."

That immediately toned him down. All he said was "Okay."

And I said, "I'm not letting you off the hook because you *didn't* train properly for these Olympics. But we're going to do this—improve your breaststroke—because that's what we can do today."

That fourth-place finish was indeed a humbling experience. The last time the world had seen Michael compete in an Olympics, in Beijing, he went undefeated: eight events, eight gold medals. Now, on Day 1 of London, he had already been vanquished. But Michael turned that defeat (if you want to call a fourth-place finish a defeat) into a positive, and over the next week he made Olympic magic again, winning four golds and two silvers.

He overcame defeat—he overcame adversity—and found success.

He proved that when roadblocks pop up during the course of your vision quest, you don't abandon everything. With the Method, I recommend not letting one failure get in the way of the dream you're pursuing.

For many non-Olympians—a working mom who on the day of a big presentation discovers that her first grader has the flu; the commuting dad who can't get home to coach his daughter's championship basketball game because of a flight delay; the high school senior whose plans to go to Stanford University just got crushed by a standardized-test score—it can be extremely challenging to stay resilient in the face of unexpected problems or setbacks.

What must you do? Two things: First, find solutions to these problems. *Working Mom:* Call your boss, explain the situation; tell him you've prepared a killer presentation, but you need to reschedule. (Most people will understand that a sick child comes before another PowerPoint talk.) *Commuting Dad:* Get on the phone to your daughter, give her the rundown on the delay, supply her with a couple of smart plays that she and her teammates can execute on the court, and tell her to do her best. She'll understand—and she'll likely play even harder to prove it. *High School Senior:* Improve your study habits (and apply to Arizona State; you'll learn as much there as at Stanford, and have more fun).

Second: Use setbacks to motivate you. Reexamine your Game Plan, refocus your intermediate goals, and, ultimately, reengage yourself in your overall vision quest.

These steps will enhance your resilience while you work through the roadblocks. Michael Phelps is an exemplar of resilience. He's motivated by failure; by Mrs. Know-it-all making a stupid comment about him; by not wanting to let people down. Anything that comes along, he turns it into motivation. There's not one stimulus that he can't use to help him be a better swimmer. He has developed an incredibly focused mind-set during the course of his career.

But resilience does not come naturally; it has to be nurtured. I've worked with a number of young swimmers whose sheer talent made them contenders in any race they entered. But, once they lost a race or faced some type of setback, they went into a funk, threatened to quit the sport and give up. I had to show them that they could bounce back. What they learned will work for you, too.

RULE 8.1: PRACTICE BEING UNCOMFORTABLE.

For all the pageantry, for all the hype, for all the heart-warming stories NBC produces during its two weeks of coverage, the Olympics, let me tell you, is a very hostile environment. The viewers at home and the fans in the stands most likely can't appreciate the setting the athletes must endure. But, having coached at the past four Games, and having seen my athletes up close in the environment, I know that the Olympics is an athlete's most grueling test.

The competition is brutal, the pressure unlike anything the athletes have ever faced. The event can be daunting, with the Games' logistics not making the situation any easier. Getting from an athlete's living quarters to his competition site is like traveling through midtown Manhattan at Christmastime: crowded, noisy, incessantly taxing. But this level of pressure and anxiety can also be anticipated. Michael and my other athletes have had to learn how to perform in these far-from-serene conditions. As such, part of our planning process is rehearsing under a "simulated pressure" that I produce for them.

How does it work? Three or four times a week, I will put my swimmers in a situation at practice where they are uncomfortable, and I expect them to rise to the occasion—or fall and have to deal with the consequences. I might put two swimmers head to head so they have to race each other. Or some days I'll get up close to a lane line and shout, "This isn't good enough. Who do you think you are?" I'm not afraid to stop practice and say, "Look, we're starting over. That's just ridiculous. That is so far beneath our standards that I will not be embarrassed by watching you swim like that."

That might sound harsh, but note that I'm not saying

they *must* do better. My message is actually subtler: It's *You can do better. Let's do it. Let's have high goals and go for them*. In suggesting this, I'm creating an environment in which they're used to performing with great expectations.

Let me give you a perfect example of how my strategy works. One day Michael and I were in Australia for a World Cup meet, a tune-up for a big international meet that was coming up. Because it wasn't a major competition, I took it as an opportunity to test Michael. Before a heat to one of his races, I intentionally stepped on his goggles and cracked them. Michael didn't notice that they were broken when he dived in for the start of the race. But as soon as he started swimming the goggles began to fill with water. True to form, Michael didn't let the malfunction affect him. He worked through the annoyance. Here's how: We have a system in our workouts by which the swimmers count their strokes when doing a lap, so that they know exactly how many strokes they need. With his leaky goggles, MP simply reverted to counting strokes to find his way to the wall and through the heat.

Later, after the race, he came over to me shaking his head and staring at his goggles. I didn't let on, only saying, "Good job. You nailed it."

Now fast-forward to Beijing and the morning of August 13, 2008. Michael dives in for the start of the 200-meter butterfly; if he wins this race, he sets the record for most career gold medals, with ten. That's all the TV announcers are chatting about; that's all everyone in the

Water Cube is buzzing about. Talk about pressure. As Michael hits the water, something goes wrong. His goggles immediately begin to fill with water. He's moving forward but, increasingly, can't see what's in front of him. He doesn't know where his competition is; he doesn't know where the wall is. "I was just hoping I was winning," he'd say later.

And yet he is coping very well, thank you. He deals with the adversity by falling back on the stroke-count method we had used in practice. He counts the number of strokes he needs to complete each lap. He eventually wins the race, and sets a world record in the process.

As we've discussed, one of my primary missions as a coach is to help my athletes strive for higher performance levels each day. Before long, the days have turned into months and then into years—and the boy who was once a promising eleven-year-old is suddenly a world-record holder. In Chapter 5, I detailed how you can achieve everyday excellence by continually resetting your goals and consistently improving your practical skill level. This process worked extremely well with Michael. He would set a performance target, I would design a program to help him reach the target, and we would work on a daily basis to get there. We knew that when we reached a new level of performance we had a platform from which to move to a higher level. Michael and I shared a desire to go beyond what anyone thought was possible. What we expected of each other made it happen.

I believe successful people—swimmers and non-swimmers alike—are much better when they regularly have that kind of "performance pressure" placed on them. So say you're a salesperson and you're planning for a major presentation that, ideally, will lead to a deal, a deal that will mean plenty for you and your company. What should you do? Well, days before the presentation rehearse it in front of a colleague, telling your partner to present you with challenges during your delivery. For instance, let her pretend to be the customer, and then midway through your talk have her call out, "Sorry, you need to cut this presentation by fifteen minutes. Something's come up. Let's wrap this baby up fast." A test under pressure.

If you can pass such stressors, you won't feel the pressure—or as much pressure—on the day of your meeting. You'll simply let the results happen.

RULE 8.2: LEARN TO DEAL WITH STRESS SO THAT YOU CAN SURVIVE OTHER CHALLENGES.

I couldn't believe what I was hearing—someone yelling louder than I could at my swimmers.

It happened in 2010, when I had traveled to Southern California to work with a group of swimmers at the U.S. Olympic Training Center in Chula Vista. One day we were invited to take part in a training program run by the Navy SEALs at their nearby base. The swimmers, who included Michael and a few other members of our national team, would go through a workout similar to what the SEALs do on a daily basis. The day started with an admiral welcoming us to the site and telling us to enjoy the course and not to worry about a single thing. "We even use nice language here," he reassured us.

The admiral had barely finished his talk and departed when some SEAL yelled out to my swimmers, "Get your asses up here!"

Our people hustled up—and kept hustling for the next four hours.

They should have known they were in trouble when they got out to the beach and saw a parked ambulance. The SEAL who was escorting us simply winked and said, "Just in case." Wearing uniforms and boots provided by the SEALs, the swimmers started the session off by running up and over a hill, down into the Pacific Ocean, where they had to briefly submerge themselves, and then back up the hill to the starting point. As soon as they returned, a SEAL shouted, "Hit the ground and roll in the sand!" The reason? So that the swimmers would have sand all over (and inside) their uniforms throughout the rest of the day, an additional discomfort to deal with.

Later routines included completing an obstacle course and a rowing exercise in the ocean. (During the latter Michael got clocked by an oar and suffered a concussion.) Throughout the whole series of events, SEALs continually yelled at their charges. My swimmers thought they were used to grueling workouts. On this day, they got a cruel awakening. Some loved the challenge, while others later told me how much they hated it.

Getting stressed was the point of the whole program. I agreed to the SEAL training program because I thought it might add to the swimmers' conditioning. The session raised their awareness of what was possible, and it put them in an unusual environment. It asked them to do things they didn't think they could do, and in situations where they had no history.

In a sense, it was a good rehearsal. In just two years, many of the same swimmers were in London and expected to perform under less than typical conditions. The Olympic Games are basically about pressure. You have to be able to do your job in the middle of a lot of noise, in the middle of a lot of yelling. By being conditioned to deal with stress, these athletes were ready to perform under the fiercest of conditions.

RULE 8.3: VISUALIZE THE GOOD THAT CAN COME FROM DISAPPOINTMENT.

One of my favorite quotes, often attributed to Winston Churchill, is this: "Success is the ability to go from one failure to another with no loss of enthusiasm." I would also say that is a pretty good definition of *resilience*. When adversity strikes, you still must take another step, you must keep going, you must swim forward . . . even if your goggles are leaking water.

Because we train every day, swimming provides the perfect laboratory to prove that maxim. When you do something so frequently, there's no way that it can go smoothly all the time. Everyone is going to experience periods when things aren't just right. So you need to develop a mind-set that allows you to fight through situations until they eventually improve.

Now, I understand. As humans, it seems that we're programmed to belabor disappointments. If something goes wrong at work, we talk about it over lunch, at the water-cooler, in the parking lot on the way to our cars. And then we continue to talk about it over dinner, with the spouse and the kids forced to listen. I've noticed that people rarely spend the same amount of time discussing the good things that happen during the day.

What I tell my athletes is this: "Don't be so hard on yourselves. If a practice—or even a race—doesn't go right, move on. Let it go."

Some swimmers, like Jessica Long, get it. Let me show you how Jessica deals with everyday pressure and disappointment. At one practice, I had the swimmers do repeats of 25 yards of butterfly. For each length, they were to take only ten to twelve strokes. I was trying to get them to gain more length from each stroke, a tactic that, ideally, will build speed and stamina. On a few laps, Jessica managed to hit the target, but more often than not she needed fourteen strokes, and in a few cases fifteen. She left practice irritated but, fortunately, not frustrated. As she told me afterward, "Bob, that was one of my favorite sets we've done. At the end of it I felt that I had learned something about my strokes—where I need to be and how I need to swim to get to that stroke count."

Of course, just qualifying for the Olympic Trials will be a big challenge for Jessica. If she makes it, the 200-meter butterfly would be an event she'd likely attempt. The pressure I put on her during practice will help in the competition. But Jessica's also self-reliant. She won't let slight failures keep her from returning the next day and going after her bigger dream. She has a way of dealing with the everyday disappointments that come along. When she's having a bad day, she says, "I visualize myself, even while I'm swimming, getting to the Trials and having people watch me as I take off my legs, watching as this girl with no legs gets in the pool and warms up and stretches. I visualize saying to myself, 'You did it! You got here!'"

To prepare to deal with and work through disappointment, consider using this exercise: Close your eyes and start thinking of something that excites you. Perhaps you see yourself in a new job or relaxing in a newly landscaped backyard or playing the piano before a sold-out audience. Pick something that speaks to you and is fun or interesting. Now, imagine that this dream is suddenly taken from you. How do you react? What's the first thing you would do? The second? The third? Whom do you call?

Think of the possible answers. Once you know them,

you will have the beginnings of a plan that will guide you through adversity.

RULE 8.4: "CANCELLATION SHOULD NOT BE CONFUSED WITH FAILURE."

Jon Stewart would appear to be the type of guy who has never felt the sting of defeat. He has been an acclaimed (and hilarious) TV-show host. A successful author. A highly praised movie producer. An A-list provocateur. All in all, he has an extraordinary record of achievement.

But one night while he was still hosting *The Daily Show*, Stewart reminisced about a much earlier, and much less successful, time in his career. It was in the mid-1990s, when he hosted *The Jon Stewart Show*, a talk show that aired (very) late into the night. After nine months of low ratings, Stewart's program was canceled—but Jon finished with a bang. For his final broadcast, he hosted a special guest, David Letterman, who rarely appeared on any program but his own. The two joked around for a few minutes, trading one-liners and barbs, until Dave shared what came across as a very poignant message. The two had been talking about the end of Stewart's show when Dave calmly said, "Cancellation should not be confused with failure."

As we now know, Stewart took that advice and ran with it—all the way to big-time stardom. He experienced defeat, learned from it, and used his knowledge to make his next TV show a huge hit.

What Dave had offered him, though, was hardly revolutionary. Essentially, he took an old chestnut and dressed it up in a new shell: Learn from your mistakes and your defeats.

However you say it, I couldn't agree with the sentiment more.

On a different scale than Jon Stewart, I've enjoyed much success during my career. I've coached national teams, been selected to the swim coaches' Hall of Fame, and worked with swimmers who have won upwards of thirty Olympic medals. In Rio come August of 2016, I will be the head coach of the U.S. men's Olympic team. Not bad—in fact, a record of achievement that I would put up against any coach in any sport. But know one thing: My failures are as numerous as my victories. Fortunately, with each one I took away more than disappointment; I gained insight, insight that I was smart enough to use toward my long-term vision.

Here's a perfect example: In 2008, shortly after Michael's historic meet in Beijing, I started coaching a thirteen-year-old swimmer named Elizabeth Pelton. At the time, Liz was considered one of the best young swimmers in the country. When I learned that I would be working with her, I thought, This is great. She's super-talented, super-dedicated, hardworking. An All-In Attitude. She's just the type of athlete every coach wants.

I was so stoked that I even went against my self-imposed edict not to make predictions. "One day," I told Michael, "this girl is going to break world records."

The thing is, I saw more in Liz than just potential. In her I saw an opportunity for me to shed the label that I could only coach MP. When I was at the University of Michigan, rival coaches would recruit against me by saying, "Bob's done a great job with Michael, but who else has he coached?"

Liz would be my validation as "a coach for all kinds." Or so I thought.

At our first big meet together—the 2010 Pan Pacific Swimming Championships in Irvine, California—Liz struggled mightily. For a girl who had trained so well in practice, she arrived at the meet with no confidence; she wasn't mentally ready to compete and failed to place in any of the events. I was so depressed after her final race that I had to leave the swimming venue briefly. I found a spot near a TV trailer, and for minutes I just sat there with my head in my hands, chiding myself: *What is wrong with you, Bowman? How did you mess this girl up? You brought her to this meet and she's clearly not ready. Maybe it's true. Maybe you can only coach Michael. You'll never be able to coach anyone else.*

Ten minutes into my self-imposed isolation, Michael came out and found me. This time *he* kicked *me* in the butt.

"Pull yourself together and get back to the meet," he told me.

In the succeeding year, Liz performed better, but only modestly. I helped her to make the World Championships team, but, again, at the big show she had a tough-luck meet. Soon afterward, she told me that she was leaving North Baltimore for another program. My ego took a hit, and I worried that my professional reputation would as well. I feared that no one would come to swim for me. I'd had a chance with this super-talented person and I couldn't get it done.

Fortunately, after a couple of days of self-pity I decided that I couldn't dwell on the disappointment and began to see what I could learn from the experience. It took some time, but, as it turned out, Liz's departure led to one of the best "teaching" moments I've had in my career. Liz eventually ended up swimming for Teri McKeever at Cal Berkeley. The roster of stars whom Teri has trained is endless and includes such decorated Olympians as Natalie Coughlan and Missy Franklin. While being coached by Teri, Liz was part of the Cal team that won a national title; she also won two gold medals at the World Championships. When I ran into Teri at a meet, I asked her how she had worked so successfully with Liz. "Bob," she said, "it's really all about the difference between how male brains react and operate and how female brains react and operate. I found out the things that were important to her, and that allowed the Liz we knew in practice to be the Liz who swam in the meets—and not a different person."

From Teri I learned that I needed to coach women, in some respects, differently than how I coach men. I've since used Teri's insight with swimmers such as Schmitty, who went on to win five medals in the 2012 Olympics, and Becca Mann, a teenager who is developing into a national star. Their success, first of all, affirms my belief that I can coach swimmers besides those named Michael Phelps. But it also reinforces my contention that failure can produce success if you choose to learn from it.

As you move toward your vision, understand that the more you can accept that failure will likely be a part of the process, the more you will be able to use it to your advantage. The political, business, and entertainment worlds are filled with stories of people who learned from their failures and then went on to fulfill their dreams. Thomas Jefferson lost to John Adams before he became president. Steve Jobs got tossed out of Apple before returning to revive the company that he'd founded. Oprah Winfrey lost her role as a newsreader at a Baltimore TV station before getting another shot with a different program, a talk show that would lead to even bigger things.

Failure is part of the Method. Sometimes it comes in waves; sometimes it catches you by surprise. But whenever it hits, understand that it is part of your pursuit. Take something from failure and use it to move your vision along.

RULE 8.5: AT ALL COST, REDUCE YOUR ANXIETIES. REALLY, AT ALL COST.

On December 14, 2014, about sixteen months after he joined North Baltimore, Tom Luchsinger published a story with his byline on the website *Outsports*. The story's headline read, "King of the Double Life: Olympic hopeful Tom Luchsinger could hide being gay from the cameras but not the mirror."

As soon as I read the article, I had a new—and better—appreciation of Mr. Perfect.

The story detailed the inner torture Tom endured as he wrestled with the decision to come out. He described nights when he was a college swimmer and he'd awaken suddenly only to toss and turn for hours, staring at his bedroom clock and saying to himself, "I have a long day ahead of me." He wrote that on nights when he couldn't sleep, he'd get out of bed and look at the medals he'd won, then upbraid himself: "Four years of accomplishments glaring back at me, titles my teammates would kill for, hold no value to me. You are still a queen. You are still a fairy!"

As I've told you already, Tom made all of my workouts, didn't let up with any set, always cheered on his fellow teammates. In practice, he seemed to do everything right. But, come the meets, he just couldn't nail it. In the summer of 2013, he had won a national championship in the 200-meter butterfly; he followed that up with a strong showing in the World Championships. But one summer later he failed to repeat the performance at Nationals and didn't make the next Worlds team. His Olympic dream was moving backward, not forward. And it was morphing into a nightmare.

"I made a deal with myself," he wrote. "If I didn't repeat

my championship title, the way I was living my life needed to change. For my own personal health, I needed to come out. I needed to accept myself and stop hating myself."

When I read Tom's piece, it made me consider how I had previously rationalized his lagging performance at past competitions. I had spent a lot of time analyzing the nuts and bolts of his swimming and the psychology of race preparation. I figured he wasn't performing well because of anxiety over the events. I hadn't considered that there may have been other causes. I hadn't moved to the next level.

Will coming out help pave Tom's way to the Olympic team? We'll have to wait until the Trials to find out. But since his article appeared I believe Tom is more at peace with himself. He's much happier, and happy people tend to succeed.

Like Tom, we all carry burdens, some of them obviously heavier than others. As a coach, I'm responsible for dozens of athletes; I want to know who they are personally and what motivates them. But in the hope of elevating their performance, can I push them to reveal secrets that might be impinging on their efforts? No, I don't think so. Boundaries do exist. But, as a mentor, as a coach, and as a leader, I do recommend that you tell the people you work with how important it is that they find someone with whom they can share any troubling thoughts. And don't just say it once. Remind them often. Let people know that, as troubles and pressure mount, having someone's ear can relieve the stress. It may not solve a problem, but it can go a long way toward easing the anxiety the problem might cause.

Consider how Tom felt when he eventually shared his story. "My friendships have gotten stronger because of my self-acceptance," he wrote. "My smile is a lot more genuine and surfaces much more frequently. I laugh a lot more. My body has time to recover from a workout because I'm actually an easy-going person. I have found qualities—both physical and emotional—that I like about myself, though that's still a work in progress. My number of good days far outnumber my bad days. I'm still the same person I have always been, just a hell of a lot better at it."

RULE 8.6: A COMEBACK SHOULDN'T BE A SOLO VENTURE.

Earlier, I told you how Michael dealt with his fourth-place finish in London; he came back and won four gold medals. In many ways, this was a great achievement. He overcame an obstacle, handled adversity, bounced back from defeat. But in light of what has happened to Michael outside of the pool, dealing with a "a fourth-place finish" may seem less than monumental.

Indeed, after his DUI incident in September 2014, Michael certainly faced a whole new level of adversity. To his credit, he realized the importance of seeking help and dealing with the issues that had led to his terrible decision. Fortunately, he had people to turn to: Peter Carlisle, his mom, his sisters, me. Yet while we were willing to help, we could offer only so much. We lacked the expertise he needed. Ultimately, Michael went to a treatment center, and over the course of six weeks he was able to get the attention he needed.

When he returned to the pool for practice, around Thanksgiving, I noticed a new person in many ways. Sure, he still came with that lanky six-foot-four-inch frame, and he still arrived at the pool with a baseball cap turned backward on his head, just as he had been doing since junior high. But, appearances aside, it was his attitude that drew my attention. I feared that he'd return downcast or sullen, especially after such a publicly embarrassing incident. Instead, he was cheerful, talkative, ready for playful verbal sparring sessions with me and the other coaches and his teammates. The fact that he was in such a better mind-set reminded me of the power we have to deal with a crisis and come back better for it.

That is, if we accept the fact that we need help.

A day or so after his arrest, Michael told his followers on Twitter, "I'm going to take some time away to attend a program that will provide the help I need to better understand myself."

Then, on December 19, about ten weeks later, and after learning much about himself in that time, he sent out a series of tweets. Among them, he said the following, "I know I still have work to do, but I have great support around me and look forward to a brighter future. I am back in the pool training and have set new goals for myself in and out of swimming for 2015 and beyond."

That's what we all need to do when adversity strikes: find help, accept help, and put the help to use. Then, when you're ready, reengage with your vision. That may mean having to reset your Game Plan and determine new goals. At first, you may find the going tricky. But understand: You won't be the first one to deal with such circumstances.

At one of his first meets after returning from treatment, in Charlotte, North Carolina, in May 2015, Michael swam terribly. He failed to place in three of the four events he raced. He'd never suffered such poor results in his career.

When I saw him after his final race, he said, "I was horrible."

I agreed, and then smiled to myself. I remembered London. Those were the same words he'd used after another race that hadn't gone so well.

History proved that things can get better.

10

RULE 9: WHEN THE TIME COMES, PERFORM WITH CONFIDENCE

"This One Was Too Close to Believe"
—THE LOS ANGELES TIMES

"Phelps Wins 7th Gold with .01 to Spare"
—THE NEW YORK TIMES

"Phelps Wins 100-Meter Butterfly Thriller to Tie Spitz's Record"
—USA TODAY

As someone who witnessed it, I can tell you that those headlines only begin to tell the story of Michael's greatest performance ever. First, let me refresh your memory of MP's fingertip, oh-so-close, "do-you-believe-in-minuscules?" victory in the 100-meter butterfly at the Beijing Games that earned him a record-tying seventh gold medal at one Olympics. Then I'll tell you how the race's result proves the value of the Method when it's finally time to go out and perform.

The story is one I've shared hundreds of times before,

at the talks I give before large groups or when I just meet random people in my travels—and it's one that I'll never tire of retelling, even when I'm older and grayer than I already am. So here goes: On Saturday, August 16, 2008, Michael faced Milorad Cavic in the final of the 100-meter butterfly. Sure, there were six other men in the race, including the American Ian Crocker, the once great though no longer dominant sprinter. But everyone knew that this was a showdown between Phelps and Cavic, an American by birth who swam for Serbia, where he also had citizenship. Through the first seven days of the swimming competition, Cavic had swum only two other races, preliminaries to the 'fly final. By contrast, Michael had competed in fifteen prelim and final races en route to six gold medals—and to near-exhaustion. His quest for eight golds, a number that would upend Mark Spitz's record of seven at a single Olympics, was alive but creaky. And that was due to the presence of Cavic. In the prelims to the 100-meter butterfly two days earlier, he had broken the Olympic record while also beating Michael.

If Michael wanted to make history, he would need to outsprint a rested and ready Milorad Cavic.

For four years, ever since the Athens Olympics ended and we had refocused our vision toward the goal of doing something unthinkable in Beijing, Michael and I had been preparing for this day. No, we didn't look past the first six events on MP's Olympic schedule. We knew they would present challenges, and, as it turned out, on Day 3 we needed a come-from-behind final leg by Jason Lezak in the 4 x 100-meter freestyle relay to secure a gold for Michael in that event.

That said, we also knew that by Day 8 of the competition MP would be almost spent, both physically and emotionally. As well, we knew that Cavic would be fresh and ready to prevent history from happening under his watch. Ultimately, we knew this would be the time for Michael to show just how capable he was of performing under the most pressure-filled of situations—and to prove the power of the Method.

The final of the 100-meters was scheduled for early that morning. Michael and I ate breakfast separately. Reason 1: I may have been thousands of miles from home, but I was still waking at 4:30 A.M. On my first day in the Olympic Village, I had found a McDonald's, and each morning that followed I was there by 5 A.M., ordering an Egg McMuffin and coffee (black) and then sitting down to read news clippings on the BlackBerry I used at the time. *Routines, routines, routines.* Reason 2: He may have been thousands of miles from home, but Michael still tried to sleep in as late as he could. *Routines, routines, routines.*

By 7 A.M., he was up, and not long afterward we were walking over to the transportation hub to get a ride to the Water Cube, just as we had on every other day of the competition. *Routines, routines, rou . . .* you get the point.

But on the walk to the bus I decided to break up the drill. You might think that on a race day Michael and

I would spend these pre-race minutes talking last-minute strategy. No chance. All the strategy talk had been conducted weeks and months before, back in Baltimore, when we were working through our Game Plan and hitting our intermediary goals. I am a firm believer in getting all the strategy work done ahead of time; that way, when you show up to perform you're not thinking about your plan. You're simply executing it.

It's a strategy that goes back to when I was in high school. If I had a test on a Friday, I would start studying on Monday; come Thursday night, I felt so prepared for the test that I wouldn't think of cracking open a book. I might catch a movie or practice the piano, but no last-minute cramming for this guy.

Back in Baltimore we had come up with a plan for the race, which would consist of two 50-meter laps of 'fly—an all-out sprint, in many ways. In 2004, in Athens, Michael had set the Olympic record of 51.25 in beating Crocker. I knew that for him to have a chance at beating Cavic he would need to be near the world mark of 50.40. The best way to do that, I told him, was "to go out in twenty-three seconds for the first lap. If you go out in twenty-three-point-anything—if you go twenty-three point ninety-nine—you win." He agreed.

That time mark was the only added ripple to this race. Otherwise, Michael would do exactly what he had been practicing for more than a decade: pulverizing the water with his dolphin kick; rhythmic breathing, head bobbing above the water every second or so; and, come the end of the race, jamming the timing pad on the wall with a powerful thrust that would leave no doubt that the race was over. In a close race, victories can be determined by how forcefully the timing pads are struck.

After being coached by me for years, years during which we had practiced slamming a wall as much as we had rehearsed dives from the starting blocks, Michael knew just the right amount of force he needed to apply. To reinforce the message, MP and I would sometimes tease each other. Every now and then I would ask, "Michael, what's *my* job?" and he would say, "To get me in the ballpark." Then I would ask, "Michael, what's *your* job?" "To get my hands on the wall." On this morning, we didn't bother with any playful exchanges. Our work was done, and Michael knew it. In fact, come performance time, my job required little more than providing him with company.

Still, before we got on the bus I did do something out of the ordinary.

During breakfast I had come across a few articles online about the upcoming race, stories in which Cavic had been quoted as saying the following: "It would be good for the sport if [Michael] lost . . . I don't usually like to put more pressure on myself than I already do, but it would be kind of nice if, one day, historians spoke of Michael Phelps winning seven golds and having the chance to win eight. And they'll talk about whoever that guy is who took it away from him. I'd love to be that guy."

When I read the quote, I thought, Interesting. I wonder what Michael might think of this.

I rarely, if ever, needed to give Michael added motivation before a race. His determination "not to lose" was usually enough incentive. But after seven days of racing, and now facing his toughest test of the Olympics, Michael, I decided, would benefit from a little fuel being added. So, as we made our way to the bus, I shared Cavic's remarks with him. Jerking his face toward me, Michael was incredulous.

"He said *what*?"

I repeated. *"It would be good for the sport if . . ."*

This time he just mumbled something.

A brushfire had been lit.

Now, let's fast-forward to the actual race, which, as I mentioned, was the greatest, most exciting, and, as it turned out, closest race of our partnership. Through the first lap, things did not look promising for Team Phelps. After 50 meters Michael stood in seventh place, Cavic leading the field. More disturbing, MP recorded a split of 24.00 seconds, a hundredth of a second off what our plan had dictated. Not good.

Over the final 50 meters, Cavic continued to lead, and I became more and more anxious. I was in the stands about 15 meters from the finish. It was a two-swimmer race when they passed me, Cavic slightly in front of Michael, with Michael furiously trying to move closer and closer and closer. *Is there enough time, enough room, for him to sneak past Cavic?* I asked myself. Now, as they got closer to the finish, I started gyrating up and around and every which way, trying to will MP past Cavic. Videos show me hopping around as if someone had dumped ice cubes down my shirt. But all my contortions did little to help. As they both reached for the wall, Cavic looked to have won the race—or so I assumed. His last stroke *seemed* to have beaten Michael's.

But then I looked up at the scoreboard. *What?* I thought. There, next to Michael's finishing time, 50.58, was OR—Olympic Record. "Great—I'm glad he's got the record," I said to myself, "but that means . . . *he WON!* Are they sure?"

In fact, the results were not official. For minutes that seemed like weeks, I kept staring at the scoreboard, waiting for the official results to appear. Finally, a murmur in the Cube, followed by a roar: The scoreboard flashed with the final—and official—results: 1. M. Phelps, USA 2. M. Cavic, Serbia. Margin of victory: .01 seconds.

Not everyone agreed with the standings. The Serbian team officials filed a protest, and probably with good reason. From TV replay angles it appeared that Cavic, who glided into the wall, had touched first. But on closer review you see Michael thrusting at the wall with his final stroke, crushing it—yes, just as he had done thousands of times during practice.

That final shove, versus Cavic's light touch, was enough to give Michael the win and, as our hometown newspaper, *The Baltimore Sun*, later reported, *"History by a hair."*

RULE 9.1: WHEN PERFORMING, DON'T FORGET THE DETAILS.

The next day Michael raced once more, in the final of the 4 x 100-meters medley relay. The U.S. team had won the event in every Olympics but one (1980, the year we boycotted the Games), and it was no different in Beijing. What made this victory special? It produced Michael's eighth gold medal, and a record that will likely stand for a very long time.

Over nine days of competition, and under enormous pressure brought on by the public, the press, me, and himself, Michael had performed with exquisite resilience, maximum skill, and unmatchable desire. How come? Because for more than a decade he had followed the Method, and with the Method the importance of resilience, skill, and desire are reinforced daily in the big and small things we do at practice. That way, I know my people are ready come performance time. As I like to tell my swimmers after a grueling workout, "Details matter. They'll make the difference when you're called on to compete."

By now you know that Michael swam thousands of meters each day. For some people, such volume might become tedious or redundant. We made sure it didn't. We used it as part of our preparation for performance day, and that gave it urgency and relevance. By reviewing and reinforcing seemingly minor details—"Michael, what's your job?" "To get my hands on the wall!"—MP was ready when he had to perform. As he showed against Cavic, he didn't need to think about closing hard. He simply did it. "If I had glided," Michael said in his post-race news conference, "I would have been way too long. I took short, faster strokes to try to get my hand on the wall. I ended up making the right decision."

By following the Method, he was prepared to perform at the biggest moment of his career and amid all the challenges that came with it.

And you will be, too.

With each intermediate goal you complete as part of the Method's Game Plan, you are learning something about yourself. That insight, combined with improved skills, will build your confidence. Collectively, those three things—skill, insight, and confidence—will help you perform when the time comes. Will you achieve success at that moment? I can't guarantee that. As I've said, I try not to predict results. And realize that on the day of a big event you may face an opponent who is simply more talented or more persuasive or smarter than you are. Or you'll go up against a situation that's more daunting or rigorous or demanding than you had imagined. Heck, you might turn out to be a Milorad Cavic and encounter a Michael Phelps, the greatest swimmer of all time, and fall short of success by the length of a cat's whisker.

And, as a consequence, you may not succeed completely in your quest.

But you will not have failed, either. You will have performed at your peak—and from that level you will have become more resilient, gained greater skills, and enhanced your desire to achieve. You will be even better prepared to move forward.

RULE 9.2: LEARN FROM PAST PERFORMANCES.

Let me show you how a previous performance can prepare you to excel at your next one.

By now we all know Michael as the Greatest Olympian of All Time (GOAT). But at his first Olympics, the 2000 Games in Sydney, he swam in just one event, the 200-meter butterfly, and finished fifth, well shy of the podium. We went to those Games, though, not expecting to medal. Michael was fifteen, the youngest American male swimmer in sixty-eight years to qualify for the Games, and he was facing men. Not surprisingly, he got beat.

Before the Games, his teammate and fellow butterflyer Tom Malchow was quoted as saying, "Michael doesn't know what it means to go to an Olympics. He doesn't know how it's going to change his life. He's going to find out soon."

Malchow was spot on. Michael and I took plenty from that performance and filed it away for future use. Little things (details, remember?), but cumulatively they can mean a lot if they're not addressed. For instance, before his prelim and semifinal races, Michael forgot to tie the strings of his bathing suit. Why? Nerves, mostly. Fortunately, nothing scandalous happened, but when we got back to Baltimore we made sure to practice the simple task of securing a bathing suit. Also, on the day of the finals I had asked him to be at the swim venue two hours before his race; that way, he would have plenty of time to relax and get into racing mood. That plan became moot when Michael arrived at the aquatic center with his roommate's credential, not his own. He had to rush back to the athletes' village to retrieve his, and got back to the pool with just sixty minutes to spare.

Michael later admitted that he "was kind of scared" during the lead-up to his first Olympic final. And rightfully so. He was a kid, with braces on his teeth and growth spurts still to come. But what he learned from that experience (and those miscues) has stayed with him. When we went to Athens four years later, he wasn't scared; he was prepared. No silly mistakes this time. And, with his confidence soaring, his race results took off as well. He won the first six of his eighteen gold medals.

When you're called on to perform, especially for the first time, look to learn as much as possible from the experience. I know, it may be difficult to think of anything *but* results. Still, try. I contend that with each experience you are strengthening your overall skill level, and thus preparing yourself for even more success down the road. I call this your "performance gain." A friend of mine knows its value. For years he sought to earn a tenured-track professorship at a major university; he had plenty of interviews and tryouts, but never a viable offer. But during this phase he continued to teach part-time at a local college. He figured that he would use this time to get the kinks out of his lectures so that when the big-time offer came he'd be ready to go. "I compare my part-time work to that of an Off-Off Broadway actor," he once told me. "With each class I teach, I am getting the mistakes out of the way. When I finally get hired full-time—when I finally make it to Broadway—I'll be ready."

I suggest that you bring a similar perspective when you're called on to perform—whether it's the first speech you give as a CEO, the first event you race as a triathlete, or the first sermon you preach as a minister. Of course, prepare with gold in mind. But if victory doesn't come, at least be sure to take something from the experience that you can use later.

RULE 9.3: STAY FOCUSED. REPEAT: STAY FOCUSED.

Scientists tell us that the brain cannot distinguish between an actual event and one that we visualize. In a sense, the act of visualizing—using our imagination to picture a goal we want to achieve—is just like watching a movie. The more "real" we make that vision, the stronger the mental picture will be when we actually attempt to attain it.

When I first had Michael write down his vision for his future, way back when he was a preteen, he had no trouble visualizing. "My dream goal is to win gold medals in the Olympics," he wrote. But then he quickly erased what he had written. I guess he said to himself, "Man, I can't put that down. I'm only twelve years old."

He flipped over the paper and scribbled, "I want to swim in the Olympics." He thought that was a more reasonable, achievable goal.

History tells us that Michael should have stayed with his first instinct. He knew, probably better than anyone else, what he was capable of, even if he was a preteen. As I've mentioned, he is the most focused person I've ever met. Come the Rio Olympics, be sure to watch him in the moments before he races. He'll sit behind his starting block, the top of his head covered by his racing cap, earbuds tucked into his ears. He'll talk to no one. His eyes will stare straight ahead at the lane he is about to enter. The Aquatic Center may be filled with fifteen thousand people, but in Michael's line of sight no one will be present. He has unquestionable focus.

Some of my other athletes aren't so lucky, and when they fail to perform in a big event focus is often the reason. My job: teach them, in the words of that old Gatorade commercial, to be like Mike when it's time to perform.

A case in point: Allison Schmitt.

At the 2012 London Games, Schmitty had a breakout performance, winning five medals. Yes, just one short of the six her teammate, Michael Phelps, had gone home with. But if you had seen Allison swim at her previous big international meet you would never have expected her to do anything in London except go sightseeing.

Here's the backstory: The 2011 World Championships took place in Shanghai. Allison was entered in several events, but the one I expected her to crush was the 200-meter freestyle, and in the preliminaries she swam exceptionally well, finishing first. In the semifinals, however, she did terribly, just eking out the last spot into the finals. When it came to the finals, it seemed Allison could not get the previous race out of her mind, and then she tried to erase the bad memory as soon as she dived off the blocks. She went out way too fast over the first 100 meters and was dead by the end. She finished fifth in a race that she could have won.

Afterward, we talked, and agreed on what the problem was: an inability to maintain her focus over a period of time, from one race to another. When we got back to Baltimore, we started working on exercises that, ideally, would improve her focus and concentration. It was not an easy skill for Schmitty to master. She's a very sociable person and she's easily distracted. I remember asking her at one practice, "What are you doing right now?" She said, "I'm talking to Michael." I went on, "What should you be doing right now?" She said, "Oh . . . warming up?" "Yes!" I told her.

By London, I was hoping that Allison had learned how to spot possible distractions—and then avoid succumbing to them.

I use Allison as an example of someone who can easily lose focus, but I fear that most of us fall into the trap, especially these days. Think of all the stimuli that regularly flood our consciousness. Family, friends, work demands, recreational needs—and that's not to mention Twitter, Facebook, Snapchat, Instagram, or the app of the moment. All these "things" can often prevent us from concentrating on the goal at hand.

For a number of years I've worked with Dr. Jim Bauman, a sports psychologist. Jim's current full-time job involves assisting athletes who compete for the University of Virginia. Prior to going to Virginia, he was a full-time senior sports psychologist with the U.S. Olympic Committee, where he began working with USA Swimming in 2004. Even after he left the USOC in 2009, Jim has continued to consult for USA Swimming. He usually travels with us to all the major competitions, such as the Pan Am Games, the World Championships, and, of course, the Olympics. Often, when I see an athlete struggling with his pre-race focus, I'll alert Jim. Although there may be a variety of sport and non-sport issues that can interfere with a swimmer's ability to focus at a competition, when it's time to race a great swimmer must be able to set all of that aside and get ready to compete. This is when Jim steps in, meeting with the swimmer and helping him focus. A typical conversation might go something like this:

JIM: "What's your job when you go out to race?"
SWIMMER: "To win a medal, to beat the guy, to win money."

JIM: "No, your job is to swim as fast as you can between point A (the start) and point B (the finish). Swimming fast has nothing to do with your opponent or a medal. It is important to focus on your job and only on what is relevant to swimming fast—your race plan and the technique of your stroke. Medals, money, your heat, your lane, other swimmers, social media, the media—they're all sources of irrelevant noise that will only slow you down. If you pull in all the irrelevant stuff, it will make things chaotic for you. Keep it simple."

To help a swimmer even further, Jim recommends that before a race the athlete write a letter, a word, or a symbol on the top of his hand or on the top of his foot—a place that is in his visual field as he prepares to race. Jim calls it a "cue," and it is intended to be a visual reminder for the athlete to stay calm and focused on the "simple" job at hand: swimming fast from start to finish. Then, in the final seconds before a race starts, a time when many athletes are most vulnerable to thoughts and feelings that might undermine their confidence, the cue becomes an immediate and available reminder for the swimmer to once again lock in on the job. It says, "Forget worrying about the swimmer in Lane 3 or the prize money at stake. Just swim!"

I've seen these cues work for my swimmers, and I've asked Jim if they can work for the non-swimmer. With little hesitation, he says, "Of course." He gives this example: "Imagine a full-time mom with four kids, and each kid is involved in a sport or some other after-school activity, and all of these activities are likely occurring in different places at the same time. Dad may be working some crazy hours, so Mom has to take on all the responsibilities of getting the kids where they need to be. Now, there may be a number of other tasks that must get done, or that it may seem necessary to get done, and this kind of demand can get pretty chaotic for one person. Plus, besides taxiing the kids all over town, Mom has one other important thing she needs to get done today—get to the grocery store—so that another critical task—feed the family later that night—can get done.

"Besides needing to be a good time and task manager," Jim goes on, "Mom could use a good visual reminder to help her complete that very important task. So she should write the letter G on the back of her hand. That way, regardless of how chaotic things might get during the day, she has the reminder—the cue—that prompts her to stop at the grocery store. The cue will tell her, 'Step back from all the chaos, take a relaxing breath, and head to the store. Task completed!'

"Sometimes," Jim adds, "we think multitasking makes us more impressive in the eyes of the world. But, in reality, if we can't effectively manage our priorities and keep them at a manageable number, we end up working very hard but decreasing the quality of our work. Compartmentalizing tasks—doing them one at a time—and utilizing a system such as cues to remind us of these tasks will not only allow us to do them but to do them well and on time. Think like a great swimmer: Aim for a quality effort by focusing on the job, what's relevant to doing your job, and eliminating the noise that is irrelevant to the job. Remove the chaos."

In the twelve months leading up to London, I stayed on Allison to remove the chaos. No, I didn't want her to become less social; Schmitty's good nature and playfulness make her a great teammate. But when it came time to practice I encouraged her to tune out the "irrelevant" conversations. At some practices, I even had Allison sit out a set, sit by herself, and visualize her stroke. Immediately, when she got back into the water, the payoff came. She seemed to have an extra bite in her swim.

Ultimately, Allison benefited in London. With each morning prelim, she knew exactly how she was going to race. With each evening final, she knew exactly how she was going to race. She was able to maintain concentration throughout the week of competition. Her trophy case is proof.

RULE 9.4: DO YOURSELF A FAVOR. DON'T CHOKE.

You've heard the old saw "Those who can, do. Those who can't, teach." Well, you'll often hear great athletes snigger among themselves, "Those who can, win medals. Those who can't, coach."

Does that saying fit me? I'd like to think I had a pretty

good swimming career. In my last year of swimming at Florida State, I finished with a personal best in the 100-yard butterfly. It was a nice note to end my career on.

That said, I do know what it's like to be an Allison Schmitt and to go out and perform—and fall short of a goal. As we just pointed out, Allison faced a failure of focus. In my case, I just simply choked when a great opportunity came my way. Let me tell you what happened.

As I mentioned earlier, when I was growing up I dreamed of one day following my hero, Leonard Bernstein, onto the stage of the New York Philharmonic and making extraordinary music. I had learned to love music at an early age, when my mom and dad got me interested in playing the piano. And, once the notes and chords and scales started to stick in my head, they fueled my desire to compose and conduct and seek out the biggest stages possible.

Then came a performance that crushed me.

Here's the situation: It's a spring day during my sophomore year at Florida State. I'm taking part in a competition in which the winners would actually conduct a symphonic band. Heading into the audition, I had said to myself, "I'm going to kill this competition." I felt that confident, that—well—cocky. But when I walked into the recording studio there was no orchestra in sight. It was just me and a professor, who, as it turned out, would judge my conducting ability while I waved my arms and a baton at orchestral music piped through speakers.

On came a recording of the Second Suite in F, by the British composer Gustav Holst. Immediately, my arms began to thrust about, jousting and jabbing as if I were Joe Frazier warming up on a speed bag. I kept this up through the entire sonata, sweat dripping down my face as the piece came to its conclusion.

With the audition over, the professor told me, "You're the most musically inclined person that's been in here today."

I said, sort of sheepishly, "Thanks," but inside I was high-fiving myself.

Then he said, "You looked like you were conducting a thousand people. You looked like Leonard Bernstein."

I left that afternoon feeling awfully good about myself.

The feeling lasted less than twenty-four hours.

The next day I went back to check the list of winners. I wasn't on it. *How's this possible? This is my future. This is what I'm going to do with the rest of my life.* I was so devastated by the news that I immediately changed my major from music to psychology.

What happened? I found out later that the professor thought I was indeed gifted, but also way too theatrical. And he was right. My job that day was to show that I— a twenty-year-old college student with some musical background—could potentially lead a college orchestra. My job was not to be the next Leonard Bernstein. I let my mind, my emotions, my big head get in the way of my practiced talent.

I choked.

You hear the term "choke" a lot around sporting events. The basketball player who misses a free throw—something he has made thousands of times before—when the game is on the line. The tennis player who double-faults during a pivotal tiebreaker. A baseball player who looks at a called third strike with the bases loaded to end a game. In another situation, these athletes would likely have performed differently. So what made these "chokeable offenses"? They came in crucial situations when the athletes felt more pressure than they normally do.

Athletes aren't the only ones susceptible to choking in pressure situations. Many a politician has said something inane during a crucial campaign debate. Top-of-their-class law students have folded under the weight of the bar exam. Even actors have been victims. Al Pacino once told the writer Claudia Roth Pierpont, "I know the terror. Absolutely. Every actor knows it. The terror of being out there and losing your concentration. The terror when you go up and you don't know your lines."

To me, choking is the inability to perform under pressure owing to psychological, not physical, reasons. It afflicts people who are usually good with an activity until the moment becomes overly demanding. They let the environment overwhelm them. They lose sight of why they're there: to simply execute what they've studied or practiced. Instead, they look ahead and become focused on outcome. They think, What happens if I don't do this?

When you face a pressure situation, stay true to yourself and your plan. Remain in the present and do what you have worked weeks and months to perfect. If you follow this prescription, the desired results should come.

Throughout his career, Michael never choked. Did he always win? No, but that was because an opponent was better than he was that day. He avoided choking because we always talked about a time goal, not a victory goal. He kept his focus on something that he could control. Sure, I might give him a range of time goals that, ideally, would lead him to gold, but we always focused on the performance.

Michael has said that he hates to lose, and he does. But what he really hates is to underperform. To get beat by someone else is one thing; to beat himself . . . well, that's inexcusable.

RULE 9.5: THE BEST PERFORMANCE COMES WHEN YOU ENJOY THE MOMENT.

I've told you a little bit about Chase Kalisz and that he may be the next great swimmer who comes from our program. While I doubt that there will ever be another Michael Phelps, I look at Chase and see a lot of similarities. Like Michael, Chase is a Maryland native. Like Michael, he has a chance to enjoy much success in the same event, the 400-meter individual medley, as MP did. And, like Michael, he brings the right mind-set when he performs.

People often liked to pitch the rivalry between Michael and Ryan Lochte as being as nasty as the one between

Auburn and Alabama or the Yankees and the Red Sox. Little did they know. Before many of their events, Michael and Ryan used to hang out together, laughing it up over some video game they were playing. They were relaxed, at ease. And the next day they performed similarly—relaxed, at ease. Chase preps for a race the same way. As he told someone one day at Meadowbrook, "Throughout the whole year I have my goals in mind. I'm always thinking about them, no matter what I'm doing. But the night before a race I stay relaxed. I'll lie in my bed, watch TV, and talk to whoever my roommate is. We'll laugh and look up some videos online. Where other swimmers are dead silent leading up to a race, I'm staying relaxed."

Take that same approach to your next performance. Look to enjoy the opportunity presented to you, not be smothered by it. Again, results are unpredictable, but I can guarantee you one thing: You will come away from a performance more satisfied if you approach it with a sense of excitement, not dread.

I often tell my swimmers that when they step on the starting block they're now on their own. I can't help them, the other coaches can't help them, their friends and families can't help them. They must rely on the work that they have put in and the confidence that they have earned through training.

My hope, though, is that those words will relax them, free them to be themselves.

A performance should be an expression of who you are.

A big part of any form of expression—whether it's in the pool, the workplace, the concert hall, or the home—is feeling free enough to be creative. Such freedom lets "the art" happen. And, as we know, the best art makes us feel good.

So relax in the moments surrounding a performance, and enjoy what you're creating.

11

RULE 10: CELEBRATE YOUR ACHIEVEMENT, THEN DECIDE WHAT'S NEXT

You've done it. You have just spent months, maybe years, working toward achieving your vision. What do you do when that moment of completion finally arrives? How do you celebrate all that you've accomplished?

Over the years we've seen Indianapolis 500 champions do cartwheels in the winner's circle and then, in keeping with some crazy tradition, down a celebratory quart of milk after they've earned the checkered flag. As far back as the 1940s, we've watched the cadets jubilantly toss their hats into the air immediately after being graduated from the United States Military Academy at West Point. We've stayed up late on New Year's Eve to listen to Guy Lombardo and then Dick Clark and now Ryan Seacrest cheer the completion of another year and all the milestones that came with it.

All achievements are unique, and so, too, should be the ways in which we commemorate them.

At least that was my thought when the greatest achievement in my career finally came to pass.

Let me set the scene: Beijing, China. Sunday, August 17, 2008. The finals of the 4 x 100-meter medley relay. An American team composed of Aaron Peirsol, Brendan Hansen, Jason Lezak, and Michael Phelps taking on teams from seven other countries. Earlier, I mentioned that the U.S. has dominated this event since its inception in 1960, so as this race is about to get started there is little suspense: the Americans will undoubtedly win. But there is drama: the fourteen thousand spectators in the Water Cube and the millions of people watching via TV in their homes or in bars or restaurants around the world are waiting to watch Michael make history.

Michael, swimming the butterfly leg (the third leg), hands off a lead to Lezak, who will finish the race and the rush for gold. Watch the replays and you can see Michael's smile getting broader and broader with each of Lezak's final strokes. MP came to Beijing with a vision: to swim world-record times so that he'd be in the position ("be in the ballpark") to win a record eight gold medals. He finished six of his first seven events nailing world records; he set an Olympic record in the other one. Now, as Lezak touches the wall for the relay win and one more world record, Michael immediately starts bear-hugging his teammates, high-fiving them, and letting the world see how happy, and satisfied, he is with his accomplishment. The Cube reverberates with what I can only describe as loudness as Michael accepts acknowledgments for what he has done.

As for me? No, I haven't swum in any race in the past nine days, but I'm still exhausted and drained and exuberant. With Michael's job done, so is mine. For eleven years we had been working together, building toward this moment—I plotting his course of action, he executing it to near-total perfection. Now he's the greatest Olympian the world has ever seen, and I am one very happy, and satisfied, swim coach.

The world's eyes are upon him, though; no one is too concerned with me, believe me. And so, with that spotlight elsewhere, I leave my seat in the Water Cube and head for a little hallway off to the side of the pool. The hallway is empty, and quiet. And for the next few minutes I stand there, at times thinking about going to my knees. And as I stand there, my face frozen in thought, my mind oblivious of my surroundings, I ask myself, *Did that really just happen? . . . Did this really just happen? . . . Did this dream really come true?*

Olympic medals are reserved for the athletes, not the coaches. No hard feelings. The athletes are the competitors. Still, I want something to commemorate this moment. Now I have it. The solitude of these few minutes are my reward for what we have just achieved.

The previous four years, during which Michael and I worked through Game Plan after Game Plan and through one set of goals and then the next, during which time we storyboarded how we might achieve history . . . and we expended so much time and mental energy . . . so many hours wondering about this and that . . . and, then, suddenly the work is done and we have what we've been seeking—world record times, history, and eight medals as well—and it is time to "celebrate."

And I find a quiet hallway and do just that, in my own way.

RULE 10.1: MAKE THE MEMORY OF YOUR ACHIEVEMENT MEMORABLE.

In that hallway, I was able to absorb—just for a moment—what we had accomplished. And, believe me, a critical part of the Method is that you have to reward yourself with a little self-absorption as payback for all the work you've done and the energy you've committed to your vision. Throughout our lives people—be they teachers, bosses, or parents—present us with tokens to commemorate a significant milestone: a good report card in grade school, a TOP SALESPERSON plaque at the end of a successful quarter or year, a watch at the end of long career, a gold medal after a very fast swim. And these tokens are nice to sneak a peek at once in a while as reminders of what we've accomplished.

But though they're fun to look at, they don't compare with the memories you take away from the moment. And only you can give yourself that.

You don't believe me? Then consider what Matt McLean once said when someone asked him about the significance of the gold medal he'd won at the 2012 Olympics: "It's just a trinket. When I look back, the medal means nothing to me, but the experiences and how they changed me as a person are rewarding. It is one of those things that you hear all the time where the journey is more important than the destination."

It may sound a bit odd, and maybe it is just a quirk in my personality, but the memory of me in that hallway with just my thoughts is one that I'll take with me forever. Why? Because of what it meant: I am there because something significant just happened, and at this point I need to stamp it in my mind.

For sure, there would be many public celebrations commemorating Michael's gold haul, and each one helped to keep the accomplishment fresh and lasting. When we arrived back in Baltimore after the Beijing Games, for instance, the city threw us a "Festival of Gold" parade, and we looped around the city waving to Michael's supporters, and they cheered the kid from "Bawlmer" for a job well done. Four years earlier, when Michael won six golds in Athens, the city threw a party that it called Phelpstival. Both events were loud, joyful celebrations. Atop our rides, Michael and I spotted people who, in some form or another, had been along for the journey to his great achievement. And we have plenty of photos from these celebrations that Michael and I will sometimes look at; they'll remind us of how people, including the two of us, were affected by our work.

But, as memorable and as upbeat as these celebrations were, I remember just as vividly the smaller events, like the party Debbie had for Michael when he retuned from Sydney after his first Olympics. Only a handful of people came that day, and there was no medal to pass around and ogle. Still, we needed to celebrate the process of actually getting to the Olympics; it was part of the original vision the family and I had put in place when we met years earlier. By following the Method, Michael had completed a part of his journey, learned more about himself, and deserved to celebrate all of that.

Over the years, I have become a firm believer in the value of celebration as part of the Method. The act, whether big or small in scale, signals that something has been completed, and with completion we have a marker of our growth. As a young coach, I can't remember being so committed to celebrations; I was probably too busy plotting out a swimmer's next vision (or my own). With the passage of time, though, I've come to realize both the importance and the joy of acknowledging achievement. For instance, in recent years I've started to celebrate the end of each year with a holiday party at my home for a hundred or so friends and family members. I don't publicize it this way, but the party's an opportunity for me and those who come—people who make my life interesting and enjoyable—to look back at all we have done singularly and together during the past twelve months.

Achieving our dream vision requires plenty of sacrifice: We use hours we can never get back, we must propel ourselves through daily to-do lists, we need to find a way to fight through emotional and physical exhaustion. But, once that moment of completion arrives, it's imperative to stop, reflect, and consider what has been accomplished and discovered. If you have found success—if you've won a championship, if you've recorded a personal best, if you've aced an important exam—you have to revel in the spirit of achievement. If success has not found you, then still celebrate the road you have been on and what you've seen along the way and learned. Remember: My Method is about the process of growth, not the results, and through the process much is still gained.

Rich O'Connor knows of what I speak. Rich isn't a swimmer; he's a former college and pro basketball player, though he didn't enjoy a highlight-filled career like Michael Jordan's or LeBron James's. As they say about players like Rich, he enjoyed his "cup of coffee" in the pros. But while he may never have won a major basketball championship, he did learn the value of going through a long season and what it brings: ups and downs and life lessons and friendships—"stuff," as Rich might say, more valuable than trophies and certainly worth celebrating any chance you can.

Later in life, after his basketball days were over, Rich transitioned into the publishing world and became the editor-in-chief of several successful magazines in New York City. The publications had small staffs, and that meant the different editors and writers and designers and photographers worked lots of long hours each month creating and assembling their products. The magazine business can be a grueling one. You complete one issue and send it off to the printer, and the next thing you know a new set of deadlines is upon you. Rich realized that such demands could turn creative work into churn work, with his staff constantly racing to beat a deadline versus reveling in the joy of "making something." So he had an idea: A day or two after a magazine had closed and left the building, he gathered his staff in a conference room for a party, a celebration. Nothing too elaborate—pizza one month, sandwiches the next. Simple, and yet oh-so-substantive.

During these celebrations, Rich would acknowledge what had just happened. "I wanted people to know what they had achieved. *You created a magazine!*" Rich says. "Not everyone can do that. They weren't stopping the world from moving, but they were doing something special. Thirty days earlier, we had set a goal—let's make a magazine—and, dammit, we did accomplish it. Before starting a new one, I wanted to make sure everyone kicked back and celebrated what they had done together."

Such celebrations work, in that they make all of us—

swimmers and writers, coaches and editors—realize that the effort we put forth has meaning, a meaning that will drive us to our next vision quest.

RULE 10.2: PLAN FOR THE QUESTION "WHAT'S NEXT?" EVEN BEFORE YOU'RE FACED WITH ANSWERING IT.

As much as celebrating is central to the completion of your vision pursuit, so, too, is the inevitable question "What's next?" Once you accomplish something—race the Boston Marathon, make partner in the law firm, get elected to run your local Parent-Teacher Association, coach a kid to twenty-two Olympic medals—either you or someone else is going to ask something in the vein of "Okay, so how do you top that?" or "Where do you go from here?" Knowing the question will hang out there, my suggestion is this: Start to think about its answer even before completing your dream goal.

Yes, the Method stresses the process of doing something, not the results of the process. Ultimately, though, there will be a result, and that means you are going to need the "next big thing" to sink your passion into. But considering this step early on doesn't mean that you should be consumed by it. You'll often hear a coach say, in the heat of a playoff run, "We're taking things one day at a time and not looking ahead." Indeed, in the final push toward a goal such words may be exactly the way a coach is thinking. But earlier in the process, when the circumstances aren't yet so intense, is when "next" should be considered.

It's then that there's some latitude for planting "the next seeds" that will blossom when you're ready for them.

I know the value of this advice, mostly because I wish someone had given it to me before I faced the biggest challenge of my coaching career.

As I've told you, after we won the eight golds in Beijing, Michael and I went through several difficult, contentious months trying to figure out how we could top such an achievement. I've already discussed how the post-Beijing period stressed our relationship. Part of the blame falls squarely on Michael. He had committed to competing in London in 2012, but for more than two years he lacked the motivation and the desire to train as he needed to. I grew more and more frustrated by his indifference to the job at hand. The by-product: Often, we went weeks without talking to each other, and when we did our conversations were mostly terse and acrimonious. Eventually, Michael came around, and we worked out our troubles, but I will never allow another athlete to treat me the way Michael did during that stretch, records and medals be damned.

That said, the period left me with emotional scars that, I must admit, were in part self-inflicted—and they can be traced to the Beijing prep years. It was during this stretch that I failed to look beyond 2008 and to consider what new priorities I might pursue once we had achieved our historic haul of gold. It was only in retrospect that I realized my mistake.

Here's what happened: From 2004 to 2008, I focused so

much of my attention on Michael and his quest that I neglected to think about developing my own skills and aptitudes. Sure, I had a vision: I wanted to elevate Michael into an Olympic hero. No problem there; that's a coach's job. But where I erred is that in pushing Michael to excel I didn't set aside the time to consider Bob Bowman the person.

Recall, this came during the period when I was also coaching the University of Michigan's men's team. So during my waking hours I was around water more than a school of dolphins is. When I wasn't plotting workouts for the Wolverines, I Game Planned for Michael's run at Mark Spitz's record. For twenty-eight hours a day—or at least that's what it seemed like—all I thought about was pools, training sets, swimsuit designs, and long-range smog forecasts for the greater Beijing area: anything that might affect Michael's Olympic pursuit. My mind ran all-Michael, all the time. So consumed was I by the effort to get Michael prepared that I neglected my own welfare. I ate poorly and put on a good bit of weight; I rarely went to a movie, a musical performance, or anything else that would have satisfied my cultural interests. I failed to stay in touch with a number of friends and family members. I failed to stay balanced, something that I told you in Chapter 8 is so essential to achieving your dream quest.

I also failed to look ahead to a time when this pursuit would be over and I would need a new challenge, one that might require me to rethink how I do things. After I returned from Beijing, I realized how I had duped myself.

Sure, we had achieved that magic eight-medal mark, but the rest of my life was very much the same. I had bills to pay, responsibilities to other athletes to fulfill, a house to maintain, swim practices to run. Essentially, I faced a sameness that I thought making history would replace.

In that period between Beijing and London, the period when Michael and I were at odds, I sought help from friends, one in particular. Greg Harden is the director of athletic counseling at the University of Michigan. In his time in Ann Arbor, Greg has worked with a number of athletes—including Tom Brady, who would go on to win Super Bowl MVPs, and Heisman Trophy winner Desmond Howard—as they tried to deal with life on and off the playing field. I had become close to Greg when I was coaching the Wolverines; we had a relationship where talking about life often made living life much easier. One day, when I was back in Baltimore, I phoned Greg to tell him about my struggles: my challenge motivating Michael and my challenge motivating myself.

Greg is a no-nonsense kind of guy, and straight up he told me that he would offer his honest opinion. "But, Bowman," he said, "are you willing to hear it?" At that moment I felt that I had no choice; I told him yes. "Okay, then, here's the deal. In our lives we periodically need to rededicate ourselves. We need to rethink who we are and what we're doing and why. Do you understand, Bowman?" I nodded through the phone. "So, Bowman, who are you? What is your sense of purpose?"

The questions shook me a bit, because for so long I had thought of myself strictly as a coach with a vision to help people swim faster. But now I was in middle age with a résumé of accomplishments but still with plenty of time to do more. At first I stumbled to answer Greg's questions, but as we talked and I had time to think about them I knew what I needed to do: find a new vision, the Game Plan to achieve it, and set new goals to help me go to the next place that I wanted to go.

Ultimately, Greg's words helped me see something: For so long, I had attached my vision to Michael's vision. I now needed to look beyond where Michael and I might go. I had to think of where *I* might go.

As I've learned, I am not alone in facing this "What's next?" crisis. In my travels I meet many men and women close to my age who have enjoyed success in their careers or satisfaction in raising their children. But one day they realize that the kids are grown and on their own or that their careers are now closer to the finish line than to the starting gate. They begin to see the necessity for developing news skills, new hobbies, new interests to keep them excited and vibrant and fulfilled.

I certainly have. Since my discussion with Greg, I feel that I've re-created myself. I travel more to Europe just for the joy of seeing the sights, not the need to attend another swim meet. I take more three- and four-day weekends during which I cultivate my other interests: my passion for thoroughbred horse racing, my dessert-baking hobby, my long-held love for music. In short, I have prepared myself for future journeys and the many goals that come with them.

Fortunately, I have not been disappointed. In recent years, a number of exciting adventures have presented themselves to me, with two of the most notable ones coming in 2015. In April of that year I was named the new head swimming coach at Arizona State University; five months later, I was chosen to coach the U.S. men's swimming team at the 2016 Rio Olympics, perhaps the most coveted job in my business. In these positions, I have discovered my next "What's next?"—with the best part being that I get to do what I've always loved to do: coach young athletes toward excellence.

RULE 10.3: KEEP A LOOKOUT FOR THOSE WHO DON'T SEE "NEXT" SO EASILY.

From the stories I have shared with you, I'm sure you can tell how much I think of the athletes I coach and the opportunity they have given me to shape their lives and their dreams. In this latest Olympic run-up, I have worked with some of the world's best swimmers, such as Yannick Agnel, Ous Mellouli, and Matt McLean. As with any coaching relationship, some develop and mature and ultimately peak. Midway through our training for Rio, Yannick, Ous, and Matt decided to leave the North Baltimore Aquatic Club to pursue different paths that, ideally, will still lead them to another Olympics. When they told me of their decisions, we shook hands and said that we looked forward to see-ing one another—and competing against one another—down the road.

Other members of the Dream Team continued to work with me toward their visions, and along the way we have tweaked their Game Plans, revised their goals, and put their All-In Attitudes toward getting them and their team-mates to perform at the highest levels possible. Tom Luchs-inger, Lotte Friis, and Chase Kalisz have been around athletics long enough to know that all the hard work they might put into a venture doesn't guarantee them a place on a podium. But, working with one another for hours upon hours each day during this Olympic cycle, they have also come to realize that much can be earned simply via the pursuit of something. Fortunately for Lotte, she's already received one reward for her excellent effort: In November 2015 she was named to her third Danish Olympic team; she's headed to Rio. As for Tom and Chase, they must wait until the June 2016 Olympic Trials for their chance to make the American team. Regardless of those results, I've learned something about the two of them. They both #deservesuccess.

Now that I'm coaching in Arizona, there is one athlete I'm certainly keeping an eye on from afar: Jessica Long. Jessica remained in Baltimore, where she is training with a very talented group of Paralympic swimmers. As we both knew when she first approached me about training with my North Baltimore swimmers, Jessica had an ambitious vision: to earn a spot at the U.S. Olympic Trials. She has made strides toward achieving that goal, but she still has a ways to go in order to finish her pursuit. Regardless, she hasn't given up the dream. "I want to get there, and I won't stop believing I can," she told a friend of mine not long ago. Believe me, I'll do whatever I can to make her wish come true—even if 2,300 miles separate us.

Then there is Allison Schmitt, a swimmer I know better than most, simply because we have been a part of each other's lives for so long. As such, I have seen her grow both as an athlete and as a person. She headed into 2016, the Olympic year, with an established record of success. Allison made her Olympic debut as an eighteen-year-old, winning a medal in Beijing when we only expected her to go there and gain a little experience for future use. Four years later, in London, she came roaring back to win five medals.

But in the summer of 2016 Allison will be twenty-six. Sad to say, that's considered old in some swimming circles. To get to Rio, Allison will face younger rivals seeking the same roster spot she wants.

And competition is not all that she must overcome.

In May of 2015, nearly three years from her glorious run in London and only fourteen months from the Rio Games, Allison admitted publicly that she had been depressed at points in the years following her 2012 Olympic success. If you know Allison (and by now you should), such an admission might seem unfathomable. She is someone with a perpetual smile who exudes warmth and cheer even on the gloomiest of days. In the decade that I have coached her, I can't think of many days when she didn't greet me with a big hello.

As it turns out, her smile only served to mask a sadness that she has felt since her achievements in London.

One day at Meadowbrook, Allison told someone that at the time of her victories, she "was on Cloud Nine. But, at the same time, I don't think I was really expecting the reaction I got afterward from friends and family and the whole community. It was overwhelming." And, of course, unsustainable. As important as celebrating an accomplishment is, it can last only so long. People need to return to their normal lives, and so, too, did Allison. But the post-London years have been challenging ones for her, as she has failed to enjoy the level of success she had previously. She and I looked for clues—a flaw in her strokes, an inability to focus on an upcoming race—and we made progress in those areas. But, as it turns out, she was dealing with something that a coach can't always see.

"Maybe the post-Olympic blues started it, and it just kept crashing down from there," Schmitty told a reporter from the Associated Press about her condition. "Or maybe it was not doing as well as I wanted to do (after the Olympics). I don't know what triggered it. . . . I didn't like that I was feeling like that. I thought if I suppressed it, it would go away. But it was something where I needed help from outside sources."

To her credit, Allison sought assistance and then shared

her story publicly. And, once she did, she began to see her form come back around. As I noted earlier, she won four gold medals at the 2015 Pan American Games, which took place just months after her public admission. That event is not nearly as prestigious as the World Championships or the Olympics, but for Allison it was a nice marker. More important, she hopes that her story will help other athletes deal with the feelings that come with success—and the demands that can come with it, too.

Allison's struggles are a reminder of the fragility of youth. As a coach for nearly three decades, I can understand the desire to push young athletes to excel; you want them to get all they can from their talents. But I've also come to realize that improvement and success shouldn't come at any cost. Yes, I want my athletes to achieve all they want, and that might mean establishing goals that can't be reached until well into the future. But in their pursuit of "this future" I also want them to learn from "the present," picking up lessons that will help them deal with life away from competition, away from the cheering, away from the question of "What's next?" I want them to feel a joy in their everyday pursuits that can be just as fulfilling as any future achievement.

RULE 10.4: DON'T GIVE UP ON GIVING SECOND CHANCES.

One day, just after it became known that Michael was planning to make a comeback and shoot for a spot in the

2016 Olympics, a reporter pestered me for a scoop in regard to Michael's competitive goals.

"Which events does Michael plan to do in Rio?" the reporter asked. "What records will he look to break?"

"Nope, can't go there," I said. "We've never talked publicly about his goals before and we're not starting now."

And I'm going to keep to that promise here—at least when it comes to swimming goals. But I am willing to share a goal I have for Michael, and it's one that has nothing to do with pools or world records or gold medals. It is all about his future when the racing truly comes to an end.

As you know, I thought that MP was done competing when he left the London Aquatics Centre that evening in August 2012. He said to me, and to the world, that he was retired, and I was certainly ready to believe that he was off on his life's next discovery.

Obviously, he wasn't. Sure, he found golf, but he didn't find fulfillment.

Throughout these pages, I have tried to share some of the glorious moments that Michael and I have experienced during our time together. Each of his victories, I feel, is a testament both to his natural ability and to the value of the Method. I have also tried, though, to be forthcoming in how I have dealt with the situations where Michael has, well, screwed up. Undoubtedly, his personal story is checkered by some serious misjudgments and reckless decisions: driving while impaired as a nineteen-year-old;

being photographed in 2009 with a bong, a picture that ended up appearing in newspapers and magazines around the world; being arrested again in 2014 for DUI and spending forty-five days in a rehab center.

With each incident, it may seem convenient to say that Michael is undisciplined out of the water, and that those closest to him, like me, have allowed him to act in an irresponsible manner. One sports columnist, Karen Crouse of the *New York Times*, wrote after his 2014 DUI, "So much of Phelps's bad behavior over the years has been enabled by people invested in him carrying his sport on his broad shoulders."

I disagree with Karen's assessment, and I've told her so. I and many of Michael's confidants long sought to prepare him for his post-swimming career. We worked with him to develop his swim school and many of his charitable causes, for instance. But, as I've come to learn, Michael just wasn't ready for this phase in his life. After London, I think he wanted to have no structure in his life and to get as far away as he could from the incredibly structured life that he had lived for so long. He wanted a freedom that few of us could handle.

As it turned out, even Michael couldn't handle it. He made, simply, some bad mistakes.

To his credit, though, he also made some smart choices, primarily reaching out for help, and as a friend I will always be there to offer that.

Right now Michael is committed to making the U.S.

Olympic team. As such, he has followed me to Tempe, Arizona, to train, to work as hard as he ever has worked, and to follow the Method to where we expect it will lead him: to very fast times in Rio de Janeiro. I do not think he is making this comeback because he was bored or because he had little to fill his days. I think he has unfinished business that he wants to accomplish in the pool. He has his goals, and some are very significant (again, I am not at liberty to share them). If he achieves them, he will further cement his reputation as the greatest Olympian of all time. I plan to make sure that he does.

But, as I have done previously, I also will use our time together to help prepare Michael for his next step, wherever that eventually does lead him. I'm treating this go-round as more of a life-skills course, in fact. We're working on getting him more involved in the business aspects of his swim school; we're getting him more involved in the day-to-day operations of his foundation. We're getting him more immersed in the goal he has always sought: to make swimming a sport for everyone.

Will Michael succeed in all these ventures? I avoid making predictions, remember? But throughout his swimming career MP has proved that the work he does today prepares him for great days tomorrow. So, as I see it, his tomorrows are looking very promising.

I propose a similar prospect to you. As you move from one vision to the next, know that there may be stumbles along the way. You might buy a business that you've eyed for years, not expecting the economy to shift suddenly downward. You might pull a hamstring days before a long-awaited cross-country bike tour, forcing you to postpone your trip indefinitely. You might just take a left when it comes to a career choice, when perhaps you should have taken a right, and you'll wonder, Why did I do that? Call them gaffes, call them blunders, call them life's miscalculations. Some may be of your own doing; others may be out of your control. When they happen, it's easy to hit the panic button and worry that a dream you may have has suddenly been extinguished.

My advice to you is this: Keep moving forward, like a swimmer with practiced strokes, and let the wisdom you've gained over time guide you. Your destination may be closer than you think.

EPILOGUE

On April 24, 2015, I did something I normally don't do: I put on a suit and tie and went to work.

As I've mentioned, most days I wake up and find the cleanest T-shirt and shorts in my dresser and the most comfortable running shoes in my closet, toss them on, and head to my office—a swimming pool. There I'll walk the pool deck barking orders and checking my stopwatch for splits and not worrying that my clothes are getting drenched from the splashes made by some of the finest swimmers in the world. My closest friends know me as a drip-dry kind of guy, not as a Brooks Brothers man.

But on this day not only had my look changed but so had my life.

That morning I was being introduced as the new head coach of the Arizona State Sun Devils swim program. It was a big day for the school, and for me. ASU wanted to upgrade a program that had become known as a perennial second-division finisher among Pac-12 Conference schools. I was the start of the school's solution.

And I wanted a new start to my life. A new challenge. A new vision.

So on this Friday morning, when ASU athletic director Ray Anderson introduced me to the press as the school's new coach, I traded my normal ensemble for a charcoal-colored suit, a white button-down shirt, and a maroon-and-gold tie, the ASU colors. In no way would this be my everyday attire, but on this day it served notice that, as I mentioned earlier, Bob Bowman had found his next big thing.

I knew of new ventures and what they can mean. In 1996, I had moved east from Napa, California, to coach with the greatest swim club in the country: the North Baltimore Aquatic Club. When I arrived there, I wasn't sure if I would ever become a world-class coach. In fact, before I accepted that job I had thoughts of quitting the sport and going to veterinary school. But I stayed committed to my passion and to my dream—to coach swimmers to world-record times—long enough to meet a very young swimmer by the name of Michael Phelps, and together we went on to do something very special. The years that followed would take me on an incredible ride: to Olympics in Sydney and Athens; to a stint as the head coach at one of the top schools in the country, the University of Michigan; and to two more Olympics, in Beijing and London. Joining me on each of these stops was Michael, who kept it all exciting and challenging by swimming races faster than most people ever thought possible.

We were a team—like Jerry Lewis and Dean Martin, Paul Simon and Art Garfunkel, Bill Gates and Paul Allen. As with those teams, Michael and I have had our contentious moments, but mostly we've enjoyed much success and shared plenty of great memories.

That said, I eventually came to realize that the Phelps-Bowman partnership could not last forever, at least not in the manner that had made it work: athlete and coach. One day, Michael would have to retire *for good*.

So I needed to look for my "What's next?"

In the desert of Arizona, I think I've found it.

"When I heard that this job was open, I'd already been thinking of my post-Michael life, which is approaching," I told the members of the press who came to report on my job at ASU. "I wanted it to be where something special could happen. I wanted to be somewhere where we could build something. This job ticked all the boxes. We're going to lay a foundation, we're going to recruit aggressively, and we're going to build over time, step by step by step."

Step by step by step. Sound familiar?

Through these "Golden Rules" I've just offered, I have tried to convey that we can all set out to be champions—in our careers, in our educational pursuits, in the hobbies we take on, and in the families we lead—but there is no guarantee that we'll reach our desired plateau. Too many obstacles exist to make such results verifiably predictable. But if you take the time to plot a route that gets you toward your goal—a step-by-step-by-step method—you're going to be, as I often tell Michael, "in the ballpark." And, once you're there, you'll be in position to make something memorable happen with the passion you possess and the preparation you've done.

Each day, I awake with the desire to help the people I work with—my coaches, my college swimmers, and my present and future Olympians—take the steps needed to realize their visions. I'm not always going to lead each one to his or her dream. My Method may not be right for a certain personality; my Golden Rules may not strike the note some people seek. I understand, and to those people I wish success in finding the method that works. But I also hold that my record of achievement ranks with the finest coaches of all time, and for that I credit the way that I do things. By taking a step-by-step approach to seeking your dream—setting a vision, designing a Game Plan, establishing and executing everyday goals, fueling and refueling your passions, and stepping up to perform—you learn more about yourself a little at a time until one day you realize who you really are: someone engaged with living a fulfilled life.

I know that strategy can work, because it has worked for me.

Today, I find myself at a very opportune point in my life.

For the second time in my career, I am a coach on a college campus, a place where people young and old come to learn. Every day that I'm here I learn something new. And, as one of the U.S. head coaches for the 2016 Olympic swimming team, I continue to prod and push the extraordinary swimmers who have oriented their lives toward excelling at the next Games in Rio. Every day they challenge me to make them better. Among these talented athletes is Michael Phelps, whom I continue to nudge and kick in the pants as he seeks to do things no other athlete has ever done, or may ever do again. Every day he makes my life a little special.

Sometimes, when I look back over my career, I chuckle. This usually happens when I recall that at one time I wanted to be a conductor of musicians. I wanted to lead orchestras as they played the finest concertos and symphonies the world has ever known. I wanted to be in a world of beauty and art. By luck or by design (or both), I've found myself, instead, leading young people in their pursuit of a dream: to swim back and forth within the narrow lanes of a pool as fast as is humanly possible. Sometimes I wonder what these swimmers look like to those who see them only when another Olympics rolls around. From their seats in a bleacher or from their couch in a TV room, spectators may view these swimmers as though they're simply rushing to get from one end of the pool to the other, using their arms and legs to churn through water faster than anyone ever thought possible.

In a sense, that image is perfectly valid.

I, however, see something more. By being on the pool deck, close to the action and next to the hearts that beat within these men and women, I see a joy that comes from pursuing a passion. I see achievement and excellence.

I see beauty, I see art.

ACKNOWLEDGMENTS

The Golden Rules may present the concepts and conventions of a celebrated Olympic swim coach, but it is the product of experiences shared among many, athletes and non-athletes alike. Here the authors (beginning with Bob Bowman) give a nod—if not a gold medal—to those who have helped shape the principles outlined in the preceding pages:

To my parents, Lonnie and Sylvia Bowman, for raising me to work hard, to do the right thing, and to respect others. And to my sister, Donna, for putting up with my crazy schedule and my loud classical music.

To my teachers—Tim Franklin, Vivian Curry, Carolyn Walters, John Bauer, Leonard and Norma Mastrogiacomo—who fueled my passion for excellence in the arts and in life.

To Ray Anderson, Dave Cohen, Deana Garner Smith, Rocky Harris, and Steve Webb, for putting faith in me and for building a culture of excellence at Arizona State University.

To Greg Harden, who taught me that being who I am is enough.

To my coaches—Scott Woodburn, Mike and Isabel Blouin, Steve Collins, Bill Shults, Terry Maul, and Sid Cassidy. You each gave me important lessons about life and sports.

To my coaching mentors—Jon Urbanchek, Murray Stephens, Paul Bergen, Teri McKeever, David Marsh, Gregg Troy, Mark Schubert, Frank Busch, Jack Bauerle, and Jack Roach—for your friendship and guidance and for challenging me to be my best.

To my faithful assistants—Keenan Robinson, Fernando Canales, Erik Posegay, Scott Armstrong, Paul Yetter, and Roman Willets. You each contributed to our success in many important ways.

To the wonderful athletes whom I have been honored to coach. All of you have shaped me as a person and as a coach. Thanks to Allison Schmitt, Erik Vendt, Scott Spann, Alex Vanderkaay, Peter Vanderkaay, Davis Tarwater, Charlie Houchin, Kalyn Keller Robinson, Eric Wunderlich, Chrissy Mitchell, and Michele Schroder for believing in me and in the process.

To our support team: Debbie Phelps (we have been a great team for twenty years!), Hilary Phelps, Whitney Phelps, Nicole Johnson, Peter Carlisle, Drew Johnson, Dr. Peter Rowe, Laisee Rintel, Marissa Gagnon, John

Cadigan, Cathy Bennett, Rich Wilkens, Jennifer Thomas, and Candi MacConaugha. You have all made our quest truly possible.

To my grandmother Helen Withers Stanton. Thanks for inspiring me to take risks and to look for the beautiful.

And to Michael Phelps, the most interesting and complex person I know. Your ability to dream, plan, and work for success has inspired a generation and redefined what is possible for the world. Your name is synonymous with excellence. Thank you from the bottom of my heart; I love you very much. The next phase of our journey is sure to be thrilling, frustrating, exhausting, and, most of all, rewarding. Keep it moving.

—Bob Bowman

To Farley Chase, of the Chase Literary Agency, who helped to conceive the idea for this book and to move it forward, and who provided continual support throughout its execution. Thanks for always lending an ear when it was most needed.

To our editors, Michael Homler and Lauren Jablonski, and their team at St. Martin's Press. You know how to make the publishing experience a pleasant and rewarding one. Your guidance has been greatly appreciated.

To Kathryn Drury, who patiently transcribed many hours of interviews, ensuring that the thoughts of Bob and his swimmers were authentic and true. Thank you so much.

To Alison Lowander, who once again showed how

a slight turn of phrase can make a very big difference. You're a wordsmith beyond words.

To the students and the faculty and the administrative staff of the School of Journalism and Communication at the University of Oregon, whose devotion to quality journalism and writing provided inspiration throughout the crafting of this book. Keep up the good fight and, as we say, "Once a Duck, always a Duck."

To Suzanne Rowe and Mark Corley, who always seemed to know when a certain writer could use a good dinner. Thank you for all the kindness you showed during a challenging stretch.

To Abby, Amy, and Judd Hark, whose good cheer sent from a continent away kept this project moving along. What good friends you are.

To John Prisco, who may not have turned a sluggish freestyler into a fast one, but you did reveal the power that comes with choosing the right word.

To the swimmers who have trained with Bob Bowman and the coaches and staff members who have worked with him. Thank you for sharing your insights on how his Method works and what he has meant to you and your careers.

To Bob Bowman, coach and confidant. You allowed a nosy reporter into your world of competitive swimming and gave him the chance to ask the hundreds of questions needed to be asked. Your record of excellence provides merit to the rules you espouse. Thank you for the opportunity to get to know you and your teaching methods. Here's to excellent results in Rio.

To all the Butlers, Kendalls, Grants, Bernsteins, Plazas, DeCaros, Lorges, Baldassares, and Abbeys. Thank you for always being good people; you are proof of the power of *the* Golden Rule.

To Claire Garvey Butler, who kept wondering how the book on "that swim coach" was going. It's all finished, Mom. A copy for you and Dad is on reserve at the Library of Heaven.

And, finally, to Ben and Leah and Sarah Butler. Thanks for letting me take the adventure that came with this project. I couldn't have asked for better teammates. Olympic wreaths are on order for each of you.

—CHARLES BUTLER

APPENDIX I

BOB BOWMAN'S RECORD
OF EXCELLENCE

1987 Graduates from Florida State University with a Bachelor of
Science degree in developmental psychology and a minor
in music composition.

1996 Becomes an assistant coach at the North Baltimore Aquatic
Center. One year later, he will begin coaching eleven-year-
old Michael Phelps.

2000 Coaches Phelps to his first Olympics, the Summer Games in
Sydney, Australia.

2001 Coaches Phelps to the first of his thirty-nine world records.
Named as an assistant U.S. coach for the FINA World
Championships.

2002 Named USA Swimming Developmental Coach of the Year.

2003 Named as an assistant U.S. coach for the FINA World
Championships.

2004 Named as an assistant U.S. coach for the Athens Olympics.
Named as head coach of the University of Michigan men's
swim team.
Coaches Phelps to six gold medals at the Athens Summer
Olympics.

2005 Named as an assistant U.S. coach for the FINA World
Championships.

2007   Named as head coach of the U.S. men's team for the FINA World Championships.

Named Big Ten Coach of the Year.

2008   Coaches Michigan to a Big Ten championship; repeats as Big Ten Coach of the Year.

Named as an assistant U.S. coach for the Beijing Olympics.

Coaches Phelps to a record-setting eight gold medals at the Beijing Olympics.

Named as the head coach of the North Baltimore Aquatic Club.

2009   Named as the head coach of the U.S. men's team for the FINA World Championships.

2010   Inducted into the American Swimming Coaches Association Hall of Fame.

2011   Named as an assistant U.S. coach for the FINA World Championships.

2012   Named as an assistant coach of the men's U.S. team for the London Olympics.

Coaches Phelps to four gold medals and two silver medals at the London Olympics.

Coaches Allison Schmitt to five medals, including three gold, at the London Olympics.

2013   Named as head coach of the U.S. men's team for the FINA World Championships.

2015   Named as the head coach of the Arizona State University men's and women's swimming program.

Named as head coach of the U.S. men's swimming team for the 2016 Summer Olympics in Rio de Janeiro.

2016   Inducted into the International Swimming Hall of Fame.

Under his guidance, Bowman's swimmers have set forty-three world records and more than fifty American records.

APPENDIX II

IN HIS OWN WORDS: THE QUOTABLE BOB BOWMAN

On Setting a Vision

"Suspending belief is necessary when setting a vision for yourself or for those you work with. You want to establish a 'reach,' and then figure out a way to reach it."

On Developing Talent

"As coaches, our job is not to keep the perfect ones and get rid of the imperfect ones. It's to try to have everybody move toward his or her potential."

"When dealing with people—especially young people who are still in the early part of their careers—you don't want to miss the chance to help them grow by giving up on them too soon. Their unrealized potential is worth all the added effort you can make to get their dreams a little closer to reality."

"I don't like the term 'performance review.' If I'm going to the trouble of planning time to meet with an athlete or an employee, I'd rather do a performance *preview*, not a review. That twist says, 'We're looking ahead, not back. Sure, let's not forget what has occurred, but let's learn from it, and let's use it to adjust our Game Plan to build for the future.'"

On the Need to Take the Occasional Risk

"To my mind, the magnitude of the achievement will be limited by your aversion to risk. Building up your risk tolerance is like building up your fitness."

"Each risk you take subsequently prepares you to take more risks, leading to a habit that more easily lets you turn visions into reality."

"Sometimes the security of our lives keeps us from living life. But if you want to take that 'next step' toward the dream you're after you'll need to become a bit riskier."

On the Importance of Goals and Working toward Achieving Them

"Achieving intermediary, progressive goals on a regular basis produces everyday excellence—and keeps your Game Plan aligned with your vision."

"Build toward a vision, don't rush to it. The progressive steps—the intermediary goals—help train your mind to deal with challenges and expectations."

On Working Daily on Your Game Plan

"Whether you are a doctor, a student, or a parent, your daily 'workout' plan is just that: a prescription for work. A coach, a professor, a boss may give you guidance or suggest a plan, but you're the one who controls it; you decide how much effort to put into something."

"It's pretty simple: The more consistency you bring to your daily goal work, the more predictable your success will be, whether you're chasing football titles, Olympic medals, or wins in your day-to-day life."

On the Value of Professionalism

"In any pursuit, you need to bring a sense of purpose to it. Because of that I want my swimmers to think of themselves as professionals with the responsibilities of a professional—that means don't miss work, be on time, do your job according to the standards expected."

"I tell my swimmers that each time they put in a little extra effort during practice they are making a deposit in their vision account. That account works like a savings account: the more you put in, the more your talent or skill will grow."

On Tracking Daily Progress

"The notes I scribble have become my daily report card, a ranking of how the day went, what I did right, and what I don't want to repeat again. You see, with 'everyday excellence,' you're attempting to be excellent *every day*. Obviously, that's not possible. But you also want to avoid repeating mistakes. My record-keeping has helped me to do just that."

"The road to reaching our ultimate vision can be a long one, the daily grind consuming us. But remember: Each day should present an opportunity to get closer to the vision, not get overwhelmed by it. A daily self-assessment will give you the needed separation from what you've just done and what you still need to do."

On Developing a Support Team

"Success in most endeavors is the product of a partnership, not the result of acting in isolation. And the beauty of such cooperation is that you get to share your success with those who have aided you."

"From supporters, look for the three In's: Instruction. Inspiration. Involvement."

"Belief. I contend that this is one of the greatest gifts you can share with others: the belief that they can succeed."

On Keeping Your Passion Fired Up

"The more you can sprinkle motivational practices into the regular vision quest, the easier it will be to keep the passion for the vision charged up."

"As you pursue your dream vision, don't let the vision become so important that you neglect other interests or fail to develop new ones. These 'secondary' skills can provide much needed perspective."

"People are emotional beings, and part of helping someone achieve a vision is understanding what motivates the person, what moves the person."

On Adversity

"I don't want my athletes to feel that failure—the inevitable lapse that comes with the pursuit of any goal—will nullify the chance to achieve what they want. That's just too much pressure, and it's pressure that will ultimately harm their growth. It depletes, rather than inspires, their passion."

"Use setbacks to motivate you. Reexamine your Game Plan, refocus your intermediate goals, and, ultimately, reengage yourself in your overall vision quest. When adversity strikes, you still must take another step, you must keep going, you must swim forward . . . even if your goggles are leaking water."

"Failure is part of the Method. Sometimes it comes in waves; sometimes it catches you by surprise. But whenever it hits, understand that it is part of your pursuit. Take something from failure and use it to move your vision along."

On Performing When Called Upon

"When you are asked to perform, especially for the first time, look to learn as much from the experience as possible. I know, it may be difficult to think of anything *but* results. Still, try. I contend that with each experience you are strengthening your overall skill level, and thus preparing yourself for even more success down the road. I call this your 'performance gain.'"

"When you face a pressure situation, stay true to yourself and your plan. Remain in the present and do what you have worked weeks and months to perfect. If you follow this prescription, the desired results should come."

On Celebrating Achievement

"I have become a firm believer in the value of celebration as part of the Method. The act, whether big or small in scale, signals that something has been completed, and with completion we have a marker of our growth."